CHALLENGES
TO PRACTICE

THE LONDON CENTRE FOR PSYCHOTHERAPY

PRACTICE OF PSYCHOTHERAPY SERIES

Series Editors
Bernardine Bishop, Angela Foster,
Josephine Klein, Victoria O'Connell

PRACTICE OF PSYCHOTHERAPY SERIES

BOOK ONE

CHALLENGES TO PRACTICE

edited by

Bernardine Bishop, Angela Foster,
Josephine Klein, Victoria O'Connell

on behalf of
The London Centre for Psychotherapy

KARNAC

LONDON   NEW YORK

First published in 2002 by
H. Karnac (Books) Ltd.
6 Pembroke Buildings, London NW10 6RE

A subsidiary of Other Press LLC, New York

British Library Cataloguing in Publication Data

A C.I.P. for this book is available from the British Library

ISBN 1 85575 282 4

10 9 8 7 6 5 4 3 2 1

Printed and bound by Antony Rowe Ltd, Eastbourne

www.karnacbooks.com

CONTENTS

EDITORS AND CONTRIBUTORS

BERNARDINE BISHOP has a background in academic English, writing, and teaching. She is a member of the London Centre for Psychotherapy and of the Lincoln Centre for Psychotherapy.

FAYE CAREY is a psychotherapist in private practice and a principal lecturer in higher education.

ANGELA FOSTER had a career in social work and higher education before training as a psychotherapist. She has a private practice and is a partner in Foster Roberts Cardona, which provides organizational consultancy and professional development services. She teaches "Consultation and the Organisation: Psychoanalytic Approaches" at the Tavistock Clinic. She has published widely in the field of mental health and co-editor of *Managing Mental Health in the Community: Chaos and Containment* (Routledge, 1998).

JOSEPHINE KLEIN was an academic for the first twenty years of her professional life and then a psychotherapist in private practice, now in the process of retiring. She is a Fellow of the London Centre for Psychotherapy and was until recently a member of the British Association of Psychotherapists. Her two most recent publications are *Our Need for Others and Its Roots in Infancy* (Routledge, previously Tavistock, 1987) and *Doubts and Uncertainties in the Practice of Psychotherapy* (Karnac Books, 1995).

VICTORIA O'CONNELL comes from a background of working with children and adolescents who have emotional difficulties and is now a psychoanalytic psychotherapist in private practice.

JOHANNA ROEBER was a teacher for the National Childbirth Trust for many years. Her two books—*Exercises for Childbirth* (co-author B. Dale, Frances Lincoln Ltd, 1982) and *Shared Parenthood* (Century Hutchinson, 1987)—came out of this work. Her work as a family therapist led her to train as a psychotherapist. Recently her work in an NHS psychotherapeutic day clinic has enabled her to develop a way of working therapeutically with disturbances between mothers and their babies.

Symposium contributors: FAYE CAREY, PRAXOULLA CHARALAMBOUS, DAVID COHEN, FELICITY CRIDDLE, ADRIAN DICKINSON, LYNETTE FRASER, MARGARET GOLDWYN, SHANAWAZ HAQUE, JOSEPHINE KLEIN, and VICTORIA O'CONNELL.

All contributors to the book are members of the London Centre for Psychotherapy.

The London Centre for Psychotherapy (LCP) has its origins in the 1950s; it became a registered charity in 1974. Its activities are threefold:

- to offer training in psychoanalytic psychotherapy (including analytical psychology) in which the leading schools of analytic thought and practice are represented;

- to organize postgraduate professional activities; and

- to provide a psychotherapy service to the community through its clinic.

The Centre is the professional association of around 200 practising psychotherapists who are registered, through the Centre, with the British Confederation of Psychotherapists.

The LCP

32 Leighton Road • Kentish Town • London NW5 2QE

Telephone 020 7482 2002/2282 • Fax 020 74782 4222

www.lcp.psychotherapy.org.uk

Registered Charity No. 267244

PREFACE

This book is the first in a series on the practice of psychotherapy. Written by members of the London Centre for Psychotherapy, it addresses situations in which classical psychoanalytic technique, without losing its integrity, is adapted to the needs of particular individuals and groups of individuals.

The contributors' professional formation equipped them with the skills and techniques required for intensive psychoanalytic psychotherapy, in which the individual patient visits a psychotherapist three or more times per week. However, as all practising psychoanalytic psychotherapists are aware, it is increasingly unlikely that we will be spending the majority of our professional lives working in this way. There are many situations in which intensive psychoanalytic psychotherapy cannot be provided, is not wanted, or is not appropriate. This poses challenges to our practice.

Each of the five chapters in this book takes up an aspect of this challenge. In an open and enquiring manner, the authors invite readers to share in their thinking as they describe how they use their psychoanalytic skills to understand the nature of particular challenges. We believe that by expressing our fears and doubts as well as our achievements we are not only describing our individual experiences but also conveying something of the culture of the London Centre for Psychotherapy, which we value as a nurturing professional environment.

In chapter one, Josephine Klein invites the reader to consider in detail the differences in technique between counselling, analysing, and something she calls "theraping". She argues that these three are distinct therapeutic activities and that the decision about which we do in the course of our work is determined by "what feels right" and by "what we feel the patient requires": "The more talent we have, and the better we have been trained, the more often we make the right decision." This valuable paper encourages us to closely examine our practice, sharpening our thinking about what we do, when, and why.

Chapter two follows on from the previous chapter, taking up the challenge of once-a-week work; it is written by Faye Carey, Praxoulla Charalambous, David Cohen, Felicity Criddle, Adrian Dickinson, Lynette Fraser, Margaret Goldwyn, Shanawaz Haque, Josephine Klein, and Victoria O'Connell, who formed a study group to explore what they thought and felt about working in this way. As they say: "All of us did some; none of us had been trained for it; we wanted to understand better what we were doing and why, and how we felt about it, and we wanted to learn from each other." Their conclusion—that once-a-week work is intensive and demanding for the therapist and requires considerable skill—would suggest that this common pattern of work should have more professional recognition and attention than it currently attracts.

In chapter three, "Singular Attention", Faye Carey makes a further contribution to this subject, offering the reader a detailed analysis of an episode of clinical work that pays particular attention to the unconscious dynamics of transference and countertransference as they emerge in once-a-week therapy.

Chapters four and five are about work in the public sector; each addresses the challenges to therapeutic practice posed by the high levels of disturbance and chaos with which a worker may be faced. Joanna Roeber, in "Has Anyone Seen the Baby?", describes some of the challenges she faces when choosing to work jointly with mothers and their babies. With careful sensitivity, she explores the pain and complexity of the unconscious three-way, three-generational dynamics in the consulting-room.

In the final chapter, Angela Foster describes her work as a psychoanalytic organizational consultant to teams working with some of the most disturbed and damaged people in our society. She analyses how the pressure of the organizational response to the "duty to care" can increase anxiety and lead to anti-therapeutic splitting, which, if not addressed, may reduce the therapeutic impact of the work and increase the danger to workers, their clients, the agency, and the general public.

CHALLENGES
TO PRACTICE

CHAPTER ONE

When we counsel,
when we analyse, when we therap

Josephine Klein

When we sing, to sing well, we have to learn to breathe from the diaphragm, open our mouths properly in a certain way, relax the throat in a certain way, and so on. That is what we do when we sing. That is not what we do when we eat, for instance. Though we open our mouths, it is not to sing but to put things in. In a day, we sing some of the time, and eat some of the time, and talk to people, spit, whistle, do many things. We do not just do one thing with our mouths.

Moreover, when we have learnt to sing, we are not obliged to sing all the time; singing is not all we can allow ourselves to do. We are not restricted to singing just because we have been trained to sing. We can still eat, talk, and so forth. The point I am making is that a person working with others in a helpful capacity may counsel some of the time and sometimes analyse and sometimes therap. All in the same hour.

The neologism "to therap" has had to be invented, not without reluctance, to distinguish counselling and analysing, both of them undeniably forms of therapy, from another therapy activity, which, for lack of a better word, may be called "to therap". There are these three distinct activities, all therapeutic, and at any moment we ought to do whichever seems appropriate. Just as whether we sing, or whistle, or eat is determined by what we want to do, so, often, whether we counsel, or analyse, or therap is determined by what feels right, by what we feel the patient requires. The more talent we have, and the better we have been trained, the more often we make the right decision. Of course, if there is a contract to do only one of these things, that has to be respected.

Deciding what the patient requires is really difficult, and it is hardly ever discussed. The initial assessment ought to give us some clues, at least on how to start off (Klein, 1998). It certainly does not depend in any simple way on what we think we see, for we have been taught how to construe the situations before us, and this tends to be what we see. There is an important paper yet to be written on *how we know what the patient needs*. In my view, since we are usually not yet in a position to know what the patient needs, we might as well start off giving patients what they want, just as a first approximation. When we understand them a bit better, we may renegotiate, or change our ways, as appropriate. Some may need theraping to start off with, some analysis, some counselling.

When we counsel

We counsel when we enable people to reflect on the situation they have asked for help with, or, to put it the other way round, when we enable people to reflect on the situation they have asked for help with, we are counselling.

We counsel when we give advice, and we have learnt not to give advice until after we have the relevant information or, if advice is asked for, not until after we have looked at the relevant information together. When we do that, we are counselling.

When we counsel, we have an obligation to stick to the client's definition of the problem, the thing the client had come for help for, in the client's view, until, perhaps, the client changes

his or her definition of the problem. This is unique to counselling: we stick to the client's request as to what we should do.

When we counsel, we extract and explore relevant information. Often we are non-directive, as Rogers (1951) taught, more
or less repeating the last three words the client said:

"... not what you wanted."

"... you stayed in the garden."

Or, summarizing rather more:

"... so he would not lend you the money."

"... so you thought it best to leave it."

Or, straightforwardly, we ask:

"And did you send the letter?"

"And who will pay the school fees?"

Or we say, in directive or negotiating mode:

"We seem to have come round to talking about your money
worries [or, your uncle, or whatever]. Do you want to stay
with that for a bit or do you want to talk more about yourself
and your marriage?" [which is what the client had come for.]

Elementary, apparently, but it seems that only students on counselling courses are taught this simple technique for keeping the
client going.

When we counsel, we are:

helping people to talk,
helping people to find the words to say it, which is part of
helping people name their feelings, which is needed for
helping people accept their feelings, which makes easier
helping people make connections conscious, and
helping people cut useless old unconscious connections and
be open to new ways of being and thinking.

[Klein, 1995, Ch. 3]

Let us imagine a woman who has come because she cannot
manage money. She earns plenty, as we know already, and we

know she makes herself only draw out spending money on Thursdays. If she runs out of spending money before then, she starves herself, does not use paid transport, does not use her plastic cards. We know she does not think this is working or is a good idea in the long run. At some point in the current session, the counsellor thinks she may be able to start thinking about her situation.

CLIENT: I am always skint by Tuesday, and sometimes already on Monday.

There is a little silence, which, of course, the counsellor hopes will encourage her to carry on, but she does not. After half a minute (this can feel very long), the counsellor says:

COUNSELLOR: You're always skint on Tuesdays, and sometimes already on Monday.

CLIENT [*quite vividly*]: That's right.

But there is another half-minute of silence, so to keep her going, he might say "How do you feel about that?" which is often useful, but the counsellor fears this might sound a bit mechanical, and also he does not want her just to say she feels awful about it and then get stuck again, so he says, quite bravely:

COUNSELLOR: What do you think that's all about?

This is brave because this is only the third time they have met and she does not know him well enough to trust him yet, and then there is the gender difference, but on the other hand it might get her thinking rather than just feeling, and the worst that can happen is that she will say she does not know. Fortunately his gamble pays off.

CLIENT: Well . . .

There is another half-minute silence but he can feel something is happening and indeed, as it turns out, her unconscious processes have turned cooperative.

CLIENT: My father says I'm spoilt.

Another half a minute.

COUNSELLOR: Your father says you're spoilt . . . [*tiny silence*].
Are you, do you think? Do you think that's it?

CLIENT: Well, not exactly, but . . .

*And it turns out that she knows what he meant by it, namely that
she is used to getting her own way. Slowly, she works it out.*

To make an end to this imaginary story, it turns out that she gets
angry whenever thwarted, angry at fate, at shopkeepers, at herself, at everyone, and that is how she feels whenever she finds
herself with the knowledge that she cannot afford something
just then, so by buying it she is defying whatever is thwarting
her, and showing them, and somehow coercing them. As it all
unwinds over the next few sessions, she laughs ruefully at herself, and she settles down to discuss how she can work better
around what she calls "this silly feeling". Note that the counsellor does not take things an inch beyond what she is willing to
explore. This is what we do when we counsel.

There is a problem, here, of professional demarcation lines.
There are now many people called counsellors working in ways
that include a good deal of theraping and analysis—in colleges,
for instance, and in doctors' surgeries. Well-trained people ap-
ply for posts as counsellors and do a good job. The important
thing for the current argument is that they are not expected to
confine themselves to counselling; they are expected, as professionals, to do whatever is technically and ethically correct to
help their clients. Counselling is not what counsellors do; counselling is what any of us do when engaged in the activity called
counselling.

When we analyse

Analysis, it must be stressed, is not the same as "what analysts
do": it is what we do when we analyse. When we analyse, we
deconstruct—"deconstruct" is the Latinate version of the Greek
word from which the English "analysis" is derived. When we

analyse, we deconstruct, we take to bits what the client is saying, and we look at the pieces, and try to look behind the pieces to see what else there is. We also analyse when we weave pieces together and construct a pattern. When we do these things, we are analysing. For that moment of time, we are "analysts".

One important way in which analysing is different from counselling is that we have no obligation to stick to the client's definition of the situation or the problem. Indeed, one might argue the opposite—we have an obligation to help uncover any deeper problems that may lie behind the current situation.

We analyse when we talk about what is not the top layer of what we hear the client saying, and moreover, we do not respond to the surface of what the client is saying. It is often a waste of time to reply to the surface. "Did you have a nice holiday?" "Do you think Uncle Herbert stole that cheque?" "Why did Mrs Bloggs slam the door in my face?" Inexperienced practitioners waste hours speculating about the motivation or whatever of people who are not in the consulting-room; the client may feel enlightened for a moment but not changed in any way. We have to train ourselves to find a range of tactful, indirect responses. "It sounds as if you are quite worried about your uncle", "That sounds awful for you (when Mrs B etc. etc.)". Or, to take a really innocuous-sounding example at length, a patient may say "Did you have a nice holiday?"—saying "Yes, thank you" is usually the easiest way of not talking about one's holiday without appearing to snub the patient. Or a patient may say:

"Oh, you have got a bad cold!"

The proper reply is:

"Yes, isn't it."

This is less mystifying or eye-catching than simply not replying, which used to be the recommended practice for analysts and psychoanalytically oriented psychotherapists. Many practitioners have given up on this because it is counterproductive. One should not respond in any detail about one's personal things because that is not the level one was hired to work at, but, except in special circumstances, one was not hired to engage in wrangles with patients about lack of good manners either. The whole point is: not to intrude into the patient's most urgent unconscious preoccupations.

Now here is a more awkward customer. The analyst may just have said "Yes, thank you" to the patient's enquiry about her holiday, but he won't let go:

"Where did you go?"

She can say "Spain" and hope that that is the end of it. Or she can stop responding and start analysing, looking at the bits below the surface. Deciding to take up the patient's curiosity about something that is not going to get him anywhere with his problems, she might say:

"It is always fascinating to know where people have been during an absence, isn't it?"

... hoping from there to get into a discussion about "Why did Mummy leave me so long?" or "Where did Daddy go when he went away?" or whatever other deep feeling may be underlying the query.

This customer is not giving up so easily, however. It is not absence that matters to him, so he does not respond to the "It's-always-fascinating . . ." gambit. It may be that he wants to win, to make her give in to his demands, it might just be about winning, in which case she has to say something like:

"You really want to win this one, don't you?"

and take it from there. Or the patient might say:

"But I want to know where *you* went."

and she:

"Yes, I see. Shall we explore why that feels so important to you?"

At that point, the conversation can go one of two ways. *Either* people can lose their temper and accuse their analyser of being too strictly professional, formal, unfeeling, heartless. These are genuine feelings with which most of us can easily identify. And

some people benefit greatly by being allowed to show how upset they are—they may have had long experience of this not
being allowed, and so the consulting-room has helped expand
their conscious experience. These upset feelings need recognizing and validating. It is by no means always best to interpret
them to the patient at this point. (Interpreting is analysing out
loud what lies beneath the surface; the practitioner thinks he is
aware of what there is but has to decide whether this is the
moment to share the insight with the patient.) *Or*, on the other
hand, the conversation may take a calmer and more obviously
analytic direction: the patient responds as requested to the
"Let's-try-to-understand" gambit, and, as the two of them listen
to the associations that arise from underground, they discover
much useful territory for further exploration. To mention a few
possible meanings they may get to:

"I love you and want to know all about you and then I shall
never lose you."

Or

"I love you and want to go wherever you've been and be part
of you that way."

Or

"Just now I have such an urgent need for friends that I want
to pretend that you're my friend and we're having a nice
chat."

Or

"You are depriving me of something, and I'm not going to be
well-mannered about it. I insist. I'm not putting up with your
refusal."

Or

"Ha ha, I've found something to embarrass you with, and
I'm not going to give that pleasure up."

Once we have established something like one of these, we can
take it from there and see how the person needed to do that just
then and how it fits into the general landscape of this particular

person. This is what makes analysing such fun. One rolls with whatever the patient is saying, to get to some underlying feeling or phantasy that needs to be addressed.

The essence of analysis is that people get to understand the connections between their behaviour and the motivations, feelings, or fantasies that underlie them. Inevitably new connections lead to re-evaluations: when analysing, we remember what the patient knows but has not in mind just now. We say:

"This reminds me of a dream you had when . . ."

Or

"This is another bout of illness just before you are due to go to France. Do you remember, this happened when you went the year before last, and also when . . ."

Or

"When the bus conductor said he would not change your fiver, there was a row. I think I remember you getting upset in much the same way when . . ."

This can be taken a stage further when the past is brought in to illuminate and make connections with the present:

"So if you had not already been vulnerable to flattery because you kept losing in competition with your sister for your parents' affection, you might not have done that thing that turned out so disastrously."

Or

"So you trained yourself to focus on physical discomfort because your mother could not listen to you when you talked about emotional feelings."

The insight gained from hearing these connections at the right time can have a very steadying effect, because people can then see a chain of causation and logic in a part of life that had seemed chaotic and perhaps shameful as well. This can give an impetus to changes in behaviour and changes in prevailing mood.

There are, however, dangers to this kind of thing, which is why one has to have a period of good counselling, good therapy, or good analysis, and preferably all three in combination, before one can be let loose on making such a connection. One danger is that circumstances prevent the surfacing of old feelings of chaos or misery or rage, closely intertwined with these connections. The surfacing and expressing of these feelings may have to be facilitated—that is the task of theraping—and if the conversation is not switched to the theraping mode at this point, the connections may remain purely intellectual. To allow these feelings to rise to consciousness requires the counsellor or therapist or analyst to know about how it feels to have them and then to recognize them in the patient and to tolerate and find words for them. If the conversation proceeds in analysing mode, much of value may be lost, at least for a time.

Another danger is that we risk incorporating our personal or cultural preferences into our remarks to our patients, who then tend to feel that we have made suggestions—as indeed we may have done—about the proper or normal way to react in stated circumstances in a particular class or ethnic subculture:

"I notice that you find it hard to say you are angry."
—that is: You should be angry now.

"You have been coming late so often, I wonder if you are fighting the therapy."
—that is: It is always your fault that you are late.

"It sounds as though you feel your husband is always right."
—that is: Don't think that your husband is always right.

Cultural influences are increasingly varied in our multi-cultured society, so until we know a lot more, our clients are probably usually better served if we ask more generally:

"How did that [event] come about?"
"What did you think it was about, that refusal [of the doctor who . . .]"
"How did it make you feel when . . ."

or more vaguely still:

"Can you tell me a bit more about . . ."

or more personally:

"How does it feel, talking to me about this?"

This leaves everyone freer, and one has a chance to learn more about other people's inner worlds.

Another great source of misunderstanding and offence has, unfortunately, to do with being trained. We draw on the great basic concepts that psychoanalysis embodies: sex, love, hate, hunger, fear, pain, need, greed. These, it has to be remembered, often operate at an unconscious level, which gives us some kind of permission to ignore the fact that the patient denies having them. In our training we are taught to look for these unconscious organizations of feelings, thoughts, and fantasies. We learn more about them from the great masters—Freud, Jung, Melanie Klein, Fairbairn, Winnicott, Bion. The danger is that the way they formulated their concepts does not always fit precisely with our own or our patients' experiences. It is now accepted that, to a greater extent than used to be allowed for, we construct our experience of reality, and these ways change over time. And fashions, too, change. From Freud's interest in fathers and penises, which analysts then naturally detected in their patient's material, through Klein's mothers and breasts, to what Bion and Meltzer have on offer just now. But not everything that any of them thought applies to everybody. We may have been taught as though it does, but it is not so. And surely we are still only at the beginning of our understanding of the human mind. All has not yet been said, and we cannot be certain what we shall find if we go further below the surface with an open mind and an open heart. There is much we do not know yet, and if we talk as though we already know all there is to know, having learnt all there is up to this moment, our patients will suffer.

Moreover, what our books and our teachers say is there may not be there in the form in which we experienced it. We may not have met those concepts in our own lives in the words, in the form, or in the context in which we met them in our training.

And if we have not, then we may not connect as deeply or imaginatively or feelingly with them as may be necessary. We hold them through a kind of alienating woolly fog, obediently because we were taught about them; and they do ring true in a way, but not in a lively manner. Their life in us does not spring spontaneously from our own familiar experience of ourselves, and this vitiates our ability to use them flexibly and imaginatively and empathetically in our contact with other people.

So we have continually to respect these grand old true-and-tried concepts and respectfully put them into the language of today and of our own experience of life, and of our patients' experience now. If we cannot, and we feel we must use our teachers' or our authors' words, we run the danger of not being as in touch with our own perceiving and conceiving selves as we could be, and our patients will be disadvantaged to that extent.

When we therap

First, to repeat two things: (a) theraping is not the same as "what therapists do"—it is what people do when they therap—and (b) when analysing or theraping, we have no obligation to stick to the patient's definition of what the problem or the situation is; indeed, one might argue the opposite, that we have an obligation to attend to issues below surface awareness.

The essence, when we analyse, is that people begin to understand the connections between their behaviour and what led to it from their inner world; getting that understanding, that insight, is the focus of analysing. Other healing processes are the focus and essence when we therap:

- acknowledgement of guilt and shame over events, past or current, now seen in a new light;
- acknowledgement of rage and pain we put up with, then or now, because we were too small or too weak to protect ourselves, or because other circumstances compelled us;

- acknowledgement of loss, past or present, and of the pain and grief that go with that.

Often the events to be acknowledged and mourned are rooted in the past, but often this is not immediately apparent to the patient who is bringing a current event. We know that history repeats itself for, as Freud said, what we do not understand we repeat. The pain of guilt, shame, rage, or loss may be brought into the consulting-room solely as happening just now, for the patient may consciously experience the event as happening for the first time now. The therapist may think it to be a repetition of something long ago that the patient has not so far been able to live through constructively, consciously, but it may not be best to confront the patient with that idea just now. Usually, if we help patients to feel their feelings about what is happening now and to understand that situation with the help of counselling and analysing techniques, we can thereafter make an opportunity to look back and explore previous manifestations of the same unhappy configuration. Therapy heals by helping the sufferer to live consciously through pains too grievous to accept at the time of injury. The techniques of counselling and analysis are meant to help ascertain the facts; the techniques of theraping give strength to accept and mourn the facts and let them be in the past.

After guilt and shame at misdeeds and errors, after shame and rage at victimization, after grief at loss, there can come a time of acceptance that the past is in the past, and people feel able to let go and respond to the present moment with less hindering luggage. The hindering luggage comprises old beliefs, old ways of looking at things, fantasies of long standing.

Part of the healing process is the acknowledgement that the past is a far-off country in which we cannot now act; we cannot change anything there, nor dwell in it. Nothing will change the past, not even revenge, hard though it is to resign ourselves to that. But there may be something in the relationship between the therapist and the suffering person that enables the sufferer to leave the past in the past, where it now belongs, and to move on. Something in the relationship may have a healing effect.

Much of the inability to let go of the past, once the past has been recalled and understood, seems to hang on the need to have one's feelings acknowledged by others, to have them confirmed, recognized. "Mirroring" is the old psychological word for it, "sharing" more everyday, "holding" and "metabolizing" more recent, "container/contained" a more frequent phrase currently. Many of the distresses we suffered, as infants, as children, or when more mature, are locked up in us like indigestible lumps, and the fact that no one cares to hear about them keeps them there, festering like abscesses. "Attention must finally be paid", says the grieving son in Arthur Miller's *Death of a Salesman*.

How can people be helped in this respect? In the conversation imagined a few pages back, where the counsellor/analyst/ therapist went on holiday and the patient seemed to want to know more about it, the counsellor/analyst/therapist who is analysing at that moment says:

> "Yes, I see, you really want to know more about me. Shall we try and see why?"

or more directly:

> "Yes, I see, I think you may be saying that you want to know because if you know all about me you can never lose me."

At which point, it was noted, one of two things could happen. Your surmise about the patient's phantasy (i.e. that he will never lose you if he knows where you are) might attract your patient's attention, and then he may move on to associations connected with that kind of phantasy—often stories about the past as they affect the present: old heartbreak, old anger, and so on. This is the more analytic alternative. On the other hand, what might be uppermost in the patient might be resentment that you would not talk about your holiday, and he might feel angry, or depressed, or withdrawn, according to the meaning your refusal has for him. Of course such feelings will have roots in the past but that is not the point just now. The point is that the patient shows what he feels, and an outpouring of feeling can do him much good. When theraping, this is what we encourage, in ways that can be stated explicitly. The essence of theraping is:

- *Behaving in such a way that people feel safe, secure, held, unlikely to feel shamed, criticized, or corrected while they let their feelings speak;*

- *Letting people cry and/or rage, letting them express their feelings more fully than is usually conventional.* We let them do this—indeed, we encourage it and do not interrupt with naff questions like "Was this in 1987?" or "Was this your elder brother or your younger one?", nor with the repetitions of what they have just said, in the theoretical language of our choice.

- *Listening and being silent, letting the other person get it all out without comment or interpretation.* Interpretation belongs to the analysis part of the work. Interpretation and comments and questions can stop this healing process and encourage people's intellectual interest rather than their ability to feel and know and express their feelings—things people have to do if they want to share their feelings and have them recognized and understood. Letting people get their feelings out in this way, listening and behaving in a way that makes a person feel safe, unlikely to be shamed, criticized or corrected, is part of the technique called "holding" (Klein, 1995, Ch. 4). Holding leads on to

- *Metabolizing.* Having another person there, who can be with you while you go over the events that hurt so much, can transform the experiences that hurt. Something changes. It sounds magical, though it should be quite commonplace to us from more familiar situations. It is what happens when a toddler has grazed her knee and you cuddle her and "kiss it better", or when you give a child that has had a burst of rage a spoonful of jam "to sweeten you again". We know it works.

Holding and metabolizing are processes that we may think of as "containing". People feel contained in treatment partly by correct analysis, partly by theraping processes. Examples of containment by correct analysis were:

> "So if you had not already been vulnerable to flattery because you were so unsuccessful in competing with your sister, you might not have taken that risk."

"So you trained yourself to focus on physical discomfort because your mother could not listen to you when you talked about emotional unhappiness."

Seeing how one thing led to another helps us to see that it would not be sensible to behave like that again, and so we gain some ego-control, containing the impulse to repeat behaviour we know is pointless. Sometimes the superego rather than the ego contains the behaviour and the moods previously under the sway of unconscious motives, but either way we can see people progressing in steering their lives as suits them better in future on the basis of what they now understand about themselves. They are containing the impulse to act on old habits, old moods.

The relationship between therapist and patient can also act as a containing process, much as children may find the courage (i.e. contain their fear) to jump into the swimming pool only when father or mother is there to watch them. The therapist may use the therapist–patient relationship as a containing process to risk an intervention that explicitly encourages the patient to make a change, to jump, to make a leap of faith;

PATIENT: "I'm so tired of being depressed all the time."

THERAPIST: "You've been saying that quite a lot recently, and I can believe it. Are you perhaps also almost saying that you wish you could change and that you feel ready to take an interest in other things than those that have been on your mind for so long? If that is so, and you try to act on it, you may feel that the depression recedes. And if it doesn't, well, we'll work on it some more until we find a better understanding, and then you can try again."

Here the therapist is indicating that patients may, as it were, make a decision to steer their attention in new directions, once they are freed from old feelings that have been acknowledged and understood and accepted, old feelings that are now ready to be contained and need no longer be allowed to poison the emotional atmosphere. This is a very delicate theoretical and practical area, because the idea of steering the attention and using what used to be called the will has had a bad press ever since Freud. Deservedly, because the will had been used so much as an instrument of repression, but using the will repressively may be seen as a misuse of a process that has its uses in more fortunate circumstances. Further discussion of this possibility must be the subject of another book. What is at issue here is the possibility of the therapist being there for the patient while the patient tries to live without the old and familiar habits of depression or anxiety, without the old obsessions, without the defences that had become habitual. Such an effort becomes feasible because the causes of the feelings or the defences have been understood, accepted, mourned, and metabolized, so that the need for them has gone, and the therapist is there as an extra resource if needed.

Still, it is a delicate matter, because we must always worry about creating a relationship with our patients that makes them feel better for a time only, and only because of us, for when they lose their relationship with us, the old feelings and the old defences may simply return. For the same reason we must avoid inadvertently, unconsciously trying to cure a person by the power of our suggestions, and there is a suspicion of that in what our imaginary therapist said just there. Granted, we have to be careful. But, it may be worth the risk sometimes, providing the element of suggestion in this example is no greater than what is often accepted in an ordinary interpretation—as in "I think you are angry because I am taking a week off", for example.

Working in the transference

Theraping is especially efficacious when we do it while the rage, grief, or other misery is still fresh, and that is why working in the transference can be such a useful technique. To a greater or lesser extent our current relationships are affected by expectations about what will happen that were built up from pre-vious experiences. We "transfer" things from the past into the present—things we have not been able to live through at the time in a way that would have helped us eventually to feel that they were behind us. Things that happened years ago and somewhere else are transferred onto our relationship with our counsellor, our analyst, therapist, bus conductor, or spouse, or Labrador dog. The process of transference happens, not only when we are working with people in a helping capacity, but whenever people interact, whether we are counselling, analysing, or theraping, or having a picnic, or bungee jumping. The issue for us when working with people is, what to do about it. Do we encourage the person to "work in the transference" or not?

We may restrict our conversation with our clients or patients so as to talk only in terms of their conscious experience. There may be an implicit contract that we do so; it is what they came for, and it would be unethical to deviate without discussing it first. At the other extreme, working in the transference may be all we have been trained for, and we treat the patient accordingly: that is, we assume as a matter of course that the relationship the patient is talking about—being slapped, borrowing money, not being willing to change a fiver—is always about us:

"The bus conductor was being awkward, and I expect you experience me as disobliging in that way as well sometimes, as when . . ."

"I think you would sometimes like to borrow what I have, and you may have felt that I was unjust when I would not share . . ."

Never seeing or referring to the transference, and seeing the transference everywhere, are extremes. Is there a way of choosing what seems right at the moment? May we choose to focus on a transferred bit or not, as seems appropriate for that person at that time? Suppose a client says:

"And then I slapped him."

In counselling mode, one might say:

"And then you slapped him"

and wait to see what the client said next. But one might say

"You are looking at me to see how I feel about that, I think."

Or

"How do you think I feel about that, I wonder."

Or

"You're wondering what it would be like to slap me, I think."

Or

"You may also have felt like slapping my face when . . ."

We need to be fairly sure that our understanding of someone's feelings or phantasies comes from our healthy countertransference and not from some neurotic unanalysed bit of our own past that we do not care to know about. Perhaps most of all we need to be sure that we are not simply drawing on our supervisor's say-so or on what we have read in a book.

There is something very therapeutic about working in the transference when we get it right, because the patients are then actually living through an old relationship that made them the people they are now. That makes it possible, at the right moment, for patient and therapist to look together at what is happening in the session, because they were both there. Thus, to go back to the wrangle at the beginning of this chapter, about where the therapist went on holiday, it is likely that the patient's emotional reaction to the analyst's unwillingness to talk about a holiday is connected with guilt or shame or pain in the past, but it is also a reality in the present. So the patient may be saying, partly because of a transference from the past:

"I love you and want to know all about you, and then I shall never lose you."

And the old desolation at loss, or the anger or confusion or worry of it, come into the present to be shared, recognized, and healed. Or if the patient meant

"I love you and want to go wherever you have been and be part of you that way"

then the desolation at loss, or anger, or confusion, or worry from that past comes into the present to be shared, recognized, healed. Or the patient may mean

"You are depriving me of something I feel I have the right to, and this time I will not put up with it."

And all the desolation at loss, and so on, and so on. Or again,

"Ha ha, I have found something to embarrass you with."

And . . .

The therapist's reception of that love, that greed, that pain, that spite, as it happened or as it is happening between the two now in the consulting-room, is therapeutic. It shows that the therapist can live with these feelings without anything terrible happening either to the therapist or to the patient. The old pain, rage, shame, guilt have been experienced, recognized, acknowledged in a vivid way.

The benefits of this way of working are obvious, and so are the dangers, which are the dangers inherent in all interpretations of patients' unconscious motivation. So much depends on whether one was correct in one's understanding of what went on unconsciously with the patient just then. Some patients do appear to need work in so focused and subjective a way a good deal of the time; others can be trained to do so. Some authorities say that we all do it all the time, and it is unconscious resistance that makes it seem so implausible. Certainly our own self-knowledge tells us that we all behave like that at times, but one can do violence to patients if one uses this focus all the time, as though patients' irritation with bus-conductors, or worries about neighbours, or hopes of exam results are never the point, really, and therefore do not need our interest.

There may be a whole spectrum: at one extreme, people who hardly relate to the therapist as a human being at all, but rather as though he or she were an unfeeling robot, not because they are in the grip of transference phenomena but because they have renounced all relating for the sake of distance or numbness. These are the patients who tell us "You are just saying that because it is your job" as though therapy is like selling cauliflowers, and selling cauliflowers is not a transaction between sentient beings. These are often people who long ago trained themselves not to feel their feelings, and they tend to think of others as like them in not "having" feelings. At the other extreme are people who suffer from what the psychiatrists of yore used to call "ideas of reference", whom we now might see as having major narcissistic traits. These are people who cannot help believing that the world revolves round them and that everything that happens has been arranged (by the therapist) with them in mind. They really benefit from transference work and little else, at least at first. In the middle between these extremes are people with easier insight into their processes.

It is a great disadvantage, when working with people, not to be aware of the transference. People in the helping professions, when not aware of these processes, can feel hurt and irritated, confused, or amused when they are accused of being stupid, venal, selfish, or of the wrong social class. Those whose training missed out on this may find it harder to deal with quarrelsome clients, or reproachful ones, or ones who find them enchanting, and find it hard to work with them constructively. They get to feeling angry, offended, insecure, flattered, or whatever the client has recruited them for. They take it personally, too uncritically. [All the same, it is worth remembering Searles' dictum, in chapter 22 of *Countertransference* (1979), that we never get accused of any flaw we are entirely clear of.]

A difficult problem is how to move in and out of work with the transference. Those who work exclusively in the transference do not have this problem, which makes this approach an attractive option, but as it does not suit all who need help, it may be too easy a way out. So this issue requires further thought and experience.

Moving from counselling mode to analysing or theraping, or from any of these modes to any other, is easier, but another question arises: is there a best order in which to work with patients, a best sequence? Counselling first? Theraping? Analysing? Not surprisingly there is no best order in which to arrange them; there does not seem to be any technique that is right for everybody at all times. There are people who come into the consulting-room for the first time and straightaway burst into tears or into long complaints, and others who sit there for hours paralysed apparently by embarrassment or an empty mind. Some people may need theraping-type healing processes before they can be in a state of mind receptive to understanding their plight. People who come after a bereavement often need help of this kind first, to sort their feelings out with someone who can share them. Others may need counselling or analysis first—they know, but in a wordless way till we give them the opportunity to find the words. Some of these are unable to cooperate with therapy-type healing processes until they have found the words to understand themselves with. Could assessors be more helpful in this respect, by finding out more about these needs before sending people on? Yes, but there is also still much that is problematic about assessing (Klein, 1998). Exciting times are ahead as theories of technique get to grips with such questions.

CHAPTER TWO

Exploring once-a-week work

Symposium with contributions from Faye Carey,
Praxoulla Charalambous, David Cohen,
Felicity Criddle, Adrian Dickinson, Lynette Fraser,
Margaret Goldwyn, Shanawaz Haque,
Josephine Klein, and Victoria O'Connell

D uring 1997 and 1998 a group of psychoanalytic psychotherapists met quarterly to explore once-a-week work.
All of us did some; none of us had been trained for it;
we wanted to understand better what we were doing and why
and how we felt about it, and we wanted to learn from each
other. We met for four or five hours at weekends. On each
occasion at least one person introduced something published on
once-a-week work that we had all read, and at least one person
introduced a once-a-week case currently being worked with.
Also a couple of people brought plenty of treats for the tea
interval. The meetings were chaired by a rather firm, well-re-
spected member, who was usually able to keep the others on the
topic. The other essential was someone who could keep good
minutes. Towards the end of the second year, everyone wrote a
page or more about their ideas, their practice, or their reading.
This chapter is a jigsaw made up of these minutes and pages,
with occasional bridging passages. Excerpts from the minutes
are quoted almost verbatim, as are excerpts from material that

the participants contributed at the end. Details of the patients' situations, dreams, and so on have been changed, but not, it is hoped, the essence of their dilemmas.

The collator has tried to find a format that would be true to the collaborative nature of the venture. The presentation is not tightly organized, and is inconclusive; we felt that the arguments had to be kept in play and that the time was right only for tentative hypotheses about the circumstances in which greater or lesser frequency might be indicated. All of us have grown through this process, and some readers may be encouraged to explore on the basis of their own experiences.

Among the points made briefly in the first meeting:

- Why is there so little written on once-a-week work? We got into a discussion on why people feel embarrassed about doing it, to the extent that they don't like to avow that they do it. There were pressures: someone's prestigious supervisor had called it "baby-sitting"; someone else's supervisor had refused to supervise a case unless the patient was made to come four times a week; we felt that there is a sense of hierarchy, with analysis five times a week being "pure gold" and less frequency a copper alloy (Freud had said so); the preference for greater frequency was a way of staring people's inequality of money out of existence—as though anyone who "really" wanted to could come more often; there is also something about people in more leisured circumstances being more able to afford five times a week as regards both time and money, and one likes to think that everyone is equally fortunate.

- We agreed, however, that we must not remain governed by such considerations or by their opposites: we must find somewhere some freedom from taking sides, for the sake of the patients as well as our own selves.

- There is resistance in the patient to more-than-once-a-week work, and there is resistance in the therapist to less-than-twice-a-week work.

- Many agreed that they are more active in commenting in once-a-week work.

- Some patients come with a problem on which they wish to concentrate, work with it for some time, feel they have come to some sort of resolution, and then go. Others, however, indicate at that point that they want to explore themselves further (i.e. they feel they *are* a problem, not *have* a problem)— like exploring a landscape, wide-ranging.

- The concept of "depth" got a thorough going-over. By what criterion is once-a-week less deep? Is deeper, more deeply unconscious? More regressed perhaps? What are the ethical implications of going more deeply into unconscious material than the patient's ailment or expectations indicate? Deeper presumably arouses more anxiety, which presumably has implications for once-a-week vs. more-than-once-a-week. Can we spell out these implications, and how important are they?

- Are more frequent sessions for the benefit more of the therapist than of the patient? (Having fewer people to hold in mind, having to work harder once-a-week, and having to bear anxiety for longer between sessions.)

- The discussion was broad, and it encompassed the wider setting in which we work; increasing numbers of counsellors being trained leading to increasing competition between counsellors and therapists, and the question of training for once-a-week work.

To anticipate, our main conclusion, of which we gradually became conscious, is that seeing people on a once-a-week basis needs as much skill, is as intense for us, and as worth while, as other work. It is certainly not easier, and certainly different. It may require a more penetrating and more rapid understanding of dynamics, more flexibility and more tact in formulating interventions, more of whatever it takes that generates an atmosphere of reverie. The qualities that more experienced practitioners develop over time may be the very ones needed for once-a-week work.

Looking at the literature

Alan Naylor-Smith's "Counselling and Psychotherapy: Is There a Difference?" (1994) was the first paper we discussed. The general reaction was that there was an unjustifiable assumption in this paper that once-a-week work was counselling and that more analytic work needed greater frequency. But in the clinical discussion two members had just presented cases that refuted this, G by holding back, and E by analysing the transference in a perfectly classical way (see next section).

Davenloo's book *Unlocking the Unconscious* (1995) came under scrutiny at the third meeting. Davenloo used confronting, anxiety-provoking techniques of interpretation. The presenter warned us that we might be shocked, as he had been, and reminded us that follow-up research had shown a high proportion of successes with once-a-week short-term work, particularly with those who showed evidence of a problem at the oedipal level of development and had little capacity to tolerate anxiety (Davenloo, 1995; Sifneos, 1972). Davenloo recommended that a careful history be taken first, where psychiatric or other counterindicators might be uncovered making this form of treatment unsuitable. He considered his technique particularly successful with highly resistant unresponsive unmotivated people, exactly the ones with whom we tend to fail.

Confronting the resistance is central to Davenloo's method. He advocates, in the first session:

1. challenging the resistance;

2. bringing into the open the intense transference feelings such challenges produce (these Davenloo calls "real feelings");

3. showing patients the relation of these transference real feelings to other aspects of their lives. (Davenloo finds that having experienced real feelings motivates patients to continue in treatment.)

It is the advent of real feelings and their place in the patient's life that "unlocks the unconscious" and facilitates further treatment.

As predicted, we were shocked and for a while in no state to look seriously at what this method had to offer. Chaos and hilarity reigned, but eventually left us more thoughtful.

Gertrude Mander reminded us that Freud had very little to say on the issue of frequency. She reported that he

> ... worked with patients every day, except Sundays and public holidays. For slight cases, or for the continuation of a treatment that is well advanced, three days a week will be enough. (Freud, 1912[e]). [Mander, 1995, p. 4]

He also felt that

> ... any restrictions of time beyond this bring no advantage to the doctor or patient, and at the beginning of an analysis they are quite out of the question [Mander, 1995, p. 4]

because of what he called "the slightly obscuring effect" that even short interruptions have on the work. There is a "Monday crust". But Mander considered that there is sufficient testimony to the usefulness of once-weekly work, even with quite disturbed patients. With the help of close supervision, she was able to hold a regressed patient through periods of primitive rage and high levels of anxiety. She also gave a telling example of another patient to whom she offered—she subsequently felt unwisely—the twice-weekly sessions he had asked for. She believed that this may have been responsible for a psychotic breakdown that followed. When they eventually returned to once-weekly sessions, this seemed to have a calming effect. The group considered that once-weekly work might suit many people like this because it challenges their defences less—defences that keep them from breaking down. On the other hand, some said that to do the work that is necessary to bring about lasting change, it is important that time and space are given in the therapy for the struggle against resistances.

Jan Harvie-Clark's "Counselling, Psychotherapy, Psycho-Analysis: A Personal Perspective" (1991), written for the *Bulletin of the British Association of Psychotherapists,* compares experiences in these three settings as they affected her when she was at the

client end of the relationship and, later, when she was the practitioner. The paper touches on once-a-week work, among other
topics. She concludes that greater frequency is sometimes but
not always necessary to achieve far-reaching changes, and that
far-reaching changes are not always what is required. The
people she really wants to argue with, rightly, are those who
insist that less frequency is always just as good, which no one in
our group would maintain. One member of our group commented:

> "In considering therapy confined to a limited number of
> sessions (usually once a week), Holmes (1998) notes that this
> creates conflict between techniques that depend on apparent
> aimlessness and the need to define goals or aims in advance.
> How does this affect once-a-week work? Most research
> shows that there is a 'tuning' of technique towards more
> focused work when sessions are limited. This means less
> opportunity for working 'without memory or desire', and it
> may mean focusing on one central dynamic only (Keller,
> 1984). Both Keller and Harvie-Clark noted that outcomes, for
> short-term work and for once-a-week work, will be limited
> by poor motivation and poor ego-strength; both believed
> that no amount of tuning of technique will surmount this.
> Both conclude, though, that once-a-week work and limited
> duration are effective for a wider range of patients than was
> previously thought. Relatively disturbed people, with long-
> standing and severe difficulties, were helped, not just those
> seeking help in a crisis.
> Jan Harvie-Clark's experience was that the more training
> you have, the better you are able to withstand transference
> projections and life/death anxiety (e.g. suicidal thoughts).
> She noted how important supervision is in this context. If we
> work many once-a-week sessions (i.e. have many patients),
> should we rethink supervision—for example, set up peer/
> other supervision or case discussions?"

Ogden's "Reconsidering Three Aspects of Psychoanalytic Technique" (1996) became very influential in our group. We liked his

concept of the inter-subjective or analytic third: Ogden considered that the best therapeutic work is done when there is what may be thought of as a joining or overlapping or merging of the unconscious processes of analyst and analysand, both in a state of reverie. Comments at the time, and later:

> "We thought that Ogden was very Winnicottian in this paper, and his 'analytic third' was Winnicott's potential or transitional space, and his 'reverie' very like Winnicott's playing."

> "Analysing v. therapy: how much playing, how much reverie, is possible at what stage of the development of the therapist–patient relationship?"

> "Is it inevitable for a relationship to become the 'analytic third' kind when two people are in a relationship? No, we all thought not."

> "Ogden allows for more active use of the analyst's counter-transference in dream-work, seeing the dream as being a product of 'the analytic dream space' and 'the inter-subjective third'. Do we think that dream-work is any different in once-a-week work? If yes, in what ways? How, if at all, is the analytic third affected by reduced session frequency?"

> "So how do we alter in our technique in once-a-week work? Ogden held that 'technique must facilitate the process'. This meant, for him, a reliance on the use of the couch over face-to-face work in order to facilitate the development of the 'inter-subjective third' (the unconscious interplay of states of reverie between patient and therapist). How difficult do we find it if our patients reject the use of the couch, and what do we do to overcome this?"

> "If we accept Ogden's view that 'the analytic enterprise is best described not by its form (including the frequency of meetings), but by its substance i.e. the analysis of transference and counter-transference (including anxiety and resistance)' (p. 887), then other differences in technique with working once a week become more peripheral."

"We liked Ogden's idea that the analytic third validated our using our 'own' associations to a patient's dreams. But we did think this was safer with patients who came more frequently, because it was easier to experience the dreams with transference and countertransference connections when patients had been to see us more recently and the patients imported less material from the surface of their lives."

"The silent patient seemed to us a rather special case. We remembered our tendency to talk more with silent than with other patients. Two of us brought instances of talking to a silent patient and thereby creating something like an analytic third almost single-handedly. At least one of us had a once-a-week patient with whom she had found this possible."

"Was furthering an 'analytic third' the most important technique? Perhaps, but we thought that some troubled people need first of all to be hanging on to a person in an other-than-reflective mode, and other troubled people have their minds too full of pressing life-problems to be able to relax at once into something more reflective. On the whole, we thought that reverie tends to come at a later stage (if at all) for quite a few patients."

"We must take into account that not only do people differ in their ability to enter easily into this kind of relationship with their therapist, but also therapists differ in their ability to generate this relationship. Some find it harder when working on a once-a-week basis, or it takes longer to establish."

"As regards the use of the couch as facilitating the development of the analytic third, we were given a striking story where the use of the couch, somehow associated with other strong pressures such as increasing the frequency of sessions, had an adverse effect on a patient, who kept wanting to leave the therapy. When the therapist freed himself from this pressure, the patient became able to be reflective and productive, and the analytic third became possible."

Illustrations from case material

*An intuition that once-a-week
is best for a patient*

G talked about her six months' work with a young man who
practised obsessional rituals and sounded oedipal, un-sepa-
rated from mother but very likely also hostile to her, depressed, with marked developmental deficiencies. G did not
feel she should see him more than once a week.

"Not only had he and the original assessor agreed on once-
a-week, he was also contemptuous of a previous experience
he had had of three-times-a-week therapy. He seemed not
psychologically minded and presented neurotic obsessional
symptoms of the kind that makes psychodynamic methods
doubtfully efficacious—cognitive work might suit him better. Given all this, G wanted to see how things went at once
a week, testing the waters. We talked about our own intuitive reasons, some of which would validate G's. For instance, the patient seemed not ready for dialogue, not being
aware as yet of his own or G's existence as people with an
inner life, and by not pushing, G was giving more time for
the transference to gather; and he was the sort of vulnerable
man who, if pressured, would become too frightened to
come to sessions; and frightened people need a lot of space
to find themselves—being proactive with them delays their
integration."

An evasive patient

"L gave an account of a very difficult woman with markedly
low self-esteem, which communicated itself to L through the
way she behaved with him: she devalued what he said, was
evasive about herself and her thoughts and feelings, did not
feel she should pay her fee, flirted instead of reflecting on
what was going on, and so forth. A typical Davenloo patient,
we thought. The first 15 months left L feeling he was not

really in touch with her or she with him. Then an incident convinced the patient that L might be willing to be in touch with her in spite of her badness. The atmosphere changed, and she was more often able to work in the sessions, be more open, take more risks, concentrate more. Now the stumbling block was rather that the transference, and indeed her usual attitude to men, was a defensive kind-of-erotic flirtatious one. And L's problem became that he did not think that she would be able to have this said to her because it was not something she could contain on a once-a-week basis. He would have to work towards greater frequency."

A patient who attacked links

"S talked about the only one of his once-a-week patients with whom there currently is a question of increasing the frequency, though she resists this and indeed is wanting to end the treatment. S was not her first therapist, and she had never felt that he was good enough for her, the perfect therapy always being withheld. Two dreams seemed to encapsulate her dilemmas in the therapy:

After a year, she was thinking of leaving and dreamt that *she was stripping wallpaper from some rooms, with an anxiety that it would weaken the walls. She uncovered some old wall paintings; one seemed to be of herself, the other of a demon.*

More recently, she dreamt that *she was in an earthquake. A helicopter came to rescue her, but she would not allow it to land for fear that it would be damaged.*"

Could such patients benefit from once-a-week work? The feeling in the group was that this patient's episodic nature demanded more continuity, and that she attacked links and might use the gaps between sessions to destroy the work. However, we also wondered whether more frequent sessions would also give her more frequent opportunities to destroy the links. There did, though, seem to be a consensus that a lot of work had been taking place in the one session per week.

A terrified young man

"O presented an initially once-a-week patient, P, who kept her at a distance for a year, with a tremendous amount of talking and no room for O to say anything. P reproached O for not doing anything. He was leading an incoherent life, clearly not in control. After a year he was able to come twice a week and also started going to the meetings of another organization, very authoritarian, anti-thinking. P liked the clarity, the structure, the sense of goals. He reproached O more than ever for not doing anything, while continuing mostly to keep her out and leading his disorganized life. He seemed to be getting more disturbed, and, after a worrying session, O suggested P come three times a week, as he seemed so ill. P's first reaction was to say that he really would go mad, but in fact he did start coming three times a week, and we decided he might have got the message from O that O could welcome and cope with his mad self and would welcome him three times as much three times a week. In the event, he brought O three of his dissociated states, experienced and symbolized in a dream, as all in a cage with him, and he reported feeling more calm."

We thought P could not have managed more than once-a-week, given the state he was in when he started, but later he was able to use more sessions with considerable benefit.

Going by the countertransference

One member of the group wrote:

"I feel that traumatic patients, patients who have had depressed mothering, need to discover an 'alive' other who can stay alive with them. This is not something that is given, this is cautiously received over time, and therefore frequency may be something that has value only when patients have discovered that someone wants to stay with them; they cannot risk being rejected, they need to leave their shell tentatively and slowly.

I have in mind a young woman who came to therapy but sat in her seat, clenching her bag, then her hands, cowering in the corner, her eyes like a vixen on my every move. If she spoke, it was never about herself, but about what was I thinking—it was unthinkable for her that I would want to sit/stay with her. She felt to me like a little girl, reared not by humans but in the wild. She had her own language, her own rules, and these rules told her not to give up what she knew. Her laws were brutal, but mine might be worse. She could not speak certain words and winced if I used them. I slowly learned these words, not through anything she might say— she said very little—but relying on how she made me feel. I felt, and had to speak, for her. She was afraid of what she could do to me and needed to know that I could protect myself, terrified she might do something that would make me banish her for ever. As she began to trust that I was not afraid of her and did not find her repulsive, she began to fear losing me.

Keeping me at a distance—one session a week—and revealing as little as possible of herself was her way of keeping me: she felt that the more I knew her, the more likely I was to end our contract or abuse her! It took three years before she could really initiate anything about herself via speech; her words are still carefully monitored by her internal censor, and although we have now increased from one to two sessions a week, her biggest fear is still that I may discover something repulsive about her and end our work. She still sits and watches, but not so intensively as she once did."

Another member wrote:

"Working with patients on a once-a-week basis does require enormous patience; one has to sit and wait for a very long time before entering a transitional space where play and reverie can take place. Children cannot play if they have to keep an eye constantly on mother. The waiting and patience communicate to such patients something that they may have never known before. Locating a mother/therapist who is there with eyes and mind, always present, will eventually lead to the symbolic other being carried internally. Then play can proceed."

Reflections and considerations

When we came to the end of our series, we knew that we had only been able to touch the fringes of a complex set of issues. We had few certainties. We could not aspire to the dignity of conclusions. To finish, each put on paper some final considerations for further thought, in the hope of keeping the issue alive in our minds and the minds of our readers.

A therapist working in a social service team wrote:

"Many patients come with very little idea of therapy. This may be because they have never had the opportunity to become psychoanalytically minded; they are not used to thinking about their feelings and/or have never made connections. Many people seem to be genuinely surprised when it is suggested that they might come more than once a week and equate this with being very 'ill'. Possibly this group of patients needs quite a long introductory period in once-a-week work.

Some patients in the NHS are single parents on benefit, and there is no question of them being able to pay for the therapy. These patients often seem to be suffering equally from emotional and financial deprivation, and the once-a-week work in the clinic is aimed at helping them reach a 'base line' from where they can begin to see themselves.

Some patients who are living with the knowledge of serious mental breakdown in the past, in themselves or in a close relative, are unwilling to come more than once a week. Perhaps this is because they fear that they will become overwhelmed if they allow the past breakdown to intrude too much into the life that they have painstakingly built for themselves.

Some patients seem to come wanting to know more about themselves, but do not see themselves as having a pressing need to solve a problem. These patients seem to settle into once-a-week quite comfortably. Some may wish for greater frequency later, some may not.

Patients who are very cut off from their feelings may find it hard to engage when they only come once a week; the therapy may perhaps remain a rather intellectual exercise or may be more easily kept in a separate 'compartment'.

If the therapist is seen as persecutory or condemnatory in the transference, it may be very difficult for any change to take place, and more frequent sessions may allow more opportunities for this to be addressed. Similarly, very angry patients may become guilty and may leave if the time between sessions is too long.

Patients who are carrying a heavy load of distress or anxiety may need a lot of time to talk about their problems; this may mean that there is little time for any development, so that patients feel they are simply 'off-loading'. More frequent sessions may give a better sense of containment.

It can be very difficult to see seriously suicidal patients only once a week because of the level of anxiety for the therapist between sessions (apart from issues of containment, etc.). Silent patients may also be difficult because it is likely that the therapist goes through long periods out of touch with the patient."

Some comments from other members:

"It seems to me that we could well have spent time discussing money and times because they are often the key factors in decisions about how often a patient will come. Perhaps cutting one's coat according to one's cloth may be therapeutic for both therapist and patient."

"There is also the important question of the training, experience, and inner resources of the therapist. There is little point in working more often in order to work 'more deeply', and thereby encourage regression, if there is not an adequate inner robustness to cope with what may come up. We have to try to be aware of our own limitations and to be as realistic as we can about what we have to offer and to whom."

"Perhaps one reason for the general reluctance to discuss or acknowledge once-a-week work is that it is actually much harder for the therapist, who needs to carry anxieties generated in the session for much longer than in work of greater frequency. It often takes more time to create a working alliance with the patient, and the use of the transference is frequently inhibited and takes longer to establish with many people. Also, there is more to remember: dreams and phantasies must be held over the week and can lose their immediacy.

Is it possible that the profession as a whole wishes to discourage this frequency of work, partly to spare the therapist—just as Freud is said to have developed the use of the couch because he found it intolerable to sit facing patients day in and day out? My own feeling is that training institutions have a responsibility to allow not only for the fact that this level of work is commonplace, but also that it requires particular effort and skill on the part of the therapist to maintain the continuity of the relationship with the patient. I would like to see a more open acknowledgement of once-weekly work as the 'bread and butter' of many therapists in private practice, and some attention given to the special conditions of this kind of work in the training of therapists."

"When this group started, I was running only a small practice. I have now been a full-time therapist for two years; I have changed, my idea of myself has changed, and although I am still in analysis, I am aware that from those changes there have been quite subtle shifts in my relation to my patients and to my practice. The first change is that I am more relaxed, having overcome two pressures. I had a rule of thumb that was to give some sort of summary or closing thought to once-a-week patients. I recognized this when one of my patients objected to it because it didn't give her time to retaliate; I realized that there was quite a lot of pressure on me and on the patient in thinking of and giving this closing thought, so I have let it drop. The second pressure was the feeling that once-a-week patients *ought* to come more often—that they and I were failing if they didn't. This second pressure has been more difficult to come to terms with, and I think is not helped by the psychoanalytic culture that we all know so well, of which Gertrude Mander writes, and which I fear many subscribe to: . . . more is not only better, but superior."

"Another significant factor is what the therapist was trained for. In psychoanalytic trainings, this is usually three or more sessions a week, and explicitly or implicitly, the sense that nothing of lasting value can be achieved on a once-a-week basis may be subtly inculcated. There is thus pressure on trainees not to raise the question of whether a psychoanalytic approach can be effective once-weekly but to damn it out of hand without further thinking. This may be partly why I like working more often. But it is also because I find the work relatively easier. Usually I find that I do not have to carry as much as I do working once-weekly. It feels as though there is more of a partnership, and I find I see patterns of relating more easily. The sessions do not feel as though I am starting over again each time. It is as if patients who can work like this are able to keep something alive between times, and I feel more able to work with them. But this is not always the case, and sometimes coming, say, twice a week can simply mean doing twice as much nothing."

"There are disturbed patients who could benefit from coming more often. They may feel threatened by what feels like the empty vastness of the week, without the contact and containment that more frequent sessions can provide. They could break down without more sessions in the week. Perhaps here we need to think about which is the greatest source of anxiety—the presence or absence of the therapist, or whom he represents?

Another important factor, I think, is what people have come to the therapy for. Do they only want only to address the acute problem that brings them to sessions? Are they able to benefit from such a focused approach, and can they return to their lives after this sort of 'pit-stop'? Or do they wish, or need as part of their experience, to find out more about themselves? And does this indicate that more frequent sessions are needed?"

"We wondered whether we needed more support and more time for shared consideration of such work, given the additional demand on our technical skill at managing beginnings/middles/endings when seeing more clients less frequently. Some thought that peer-group case-discussions or supervisions targeted at once-a-week work would offer much, including further thinking on technique."

"I would like to emphasize the importance of our unanimous observation that there was a measure of denial in the profession with regard to the large number of people who do this work, and its importance both to practitioners and to patients who for a variety of reasons are unwilling or unable to come more often. It seems almost as if once-weekly work could be persuaded to go away by being ignored or being treated as unimportant. It is, after all, the basis of work in the Health Service, and a substantial number of patients seen in private practice come only once a week. Could it be that our profession has such difficulty with external realities that this particular one is impossible to acknowledge?"

At our final meeting—to consider a first draft of this chapter—we found ourselves formulating the feelings that had led us to work with such fervour on this subject. Foremost was our sense that this important aspect of our work was quite unsuitably devalued in our profession. Why, asked someone, when most of our teachers also see once-a-week patients, do they hardly ever refer to them? Why is three-or-more taken for granted as the only context of our work when we all know it is not?

In the discussion we found ourselves struggling with a tendency to regard once-a-week work as "just as good", or "better", as well as "not as good", when consciously we had already several times concluded that it was *different in respects we were trying to understand.*

Our professional culture, in that it devalues once-a-week work, tends to make us feel like inferior junior members whenever we see a patient on a once-a-week basis, and, consciously or unconsciously, there is a pressure to feel that as we get to be more senior, we shall be doing less of it. Indeed, seniority in the profession is to some extent gauged by the number of three-/four-/five-times patients we have. Our profession does not help us to feel contained in this aspect of our work.

We became conscious of interprofessional political implications. Although it seems now generally acknowledged that counselling is not a lesser kind of psychotherapy but a valuable process in its own right, there is something about once-a-week work that easily tempts people to confuse the two, and that, in our professional culture, also devalues the work.

We realized with some shame that to the extent that our professional culture diminishes respect for once-a-week work, not only do we feel diminished when we come to engage in it, but the patient who comes once a week is at risk of being diminished.

There are also implications in this as regards the assessment of patients. How do we actually know that once-a-week is "enough" or "not enough"? Where is our explicit thinking about this? What are the implications if we think that once-a-week is all a patient is capable of?

Consciously or unconsciously, people trained on a three-times-a-week basis feel diminished by the once-a-week work they do—that may be why it is rarely mentioned in the culture and why little interest is shown in doing it well—we try not to think about it as a special topic. We discovered a parallel with the way the role of the father is so often denied in therapy—we concentrate on mother–child interaction. Yet the father is very much part of the family, and he is often the breadwinner. For many of us, once-a-week work is our breadwinner, but invisible, taken for granted, not to be made much of.

Our main conclusion, which we only gradually came to in a conscious way, is that seeing people on a once-a-week basis needs as much skill, is as intense for us, and as worth while as other work. It should not be assumed that it is all right for beginners. It requires a more penetrating and more rapid and accurate understanding of dynamics, more flexibility, and easier access to tactful language in formulating interventions, more of whatever it takes that generates an atmosphere of common reverie. (Chapter 3, by Faye Carey, has more to say about all these issues.) Once-a-week work is different. We do it of necessity at present, without special training or encouragement. Special training is needed for the special skills required. What these skills are needs further definition and exploration. We are left hoping that our small beginnings in the group may prove to be the start of a more comprehensive debate.

CHAPTER THREE

Singular attention:
some once-a-week therapies

Faye Carey

Mark, who is in his mid–30s, returned to our once-weekly sessions following a three-week spring break, sat down, smiled, and said that he had expected to come to the door and find that I might not have remembered that this was the day he would be returning.

He clarified this by saying that he knew *he'd* got it right (at the time of the previous break he'd been very anxious that he'd got it wrong), but worried that this time *I* may have forgotten yet would somehow hold him responsible. He thereby managed to communicate to me a perception of an object that is both unreliable and punitive. All this was said as a sort of introductory aside, a form of greeting.

As there had been no uncertainty prior to the break regarding the arrangements concerning the return to the sessions, my feeling was that his anxiety was something that had developed over—possibly as a result of—the break. I first wondered whether the separation had activated a belief that he is forgettable, and did the fantasy indicate a form of reversal whereby I become negligent and forgetful? Feeling forgotten—where the other is at fault—must, after all, be preferable to feeling forgettable. This fantasy seemed quickly to gain the status of conviction, strengthened by the belief that he would now have to cope with my negligence by needing to be compliant in the face of my anticipated denial, thereby allowing him to feel doubly victimized. Was the communication therefore intended to reinforce this reversal, by making me feel guilty? The idea of reversal stimulated a further thought in me: perhaps it was he who was feeling guilty? Was he anxious that it is *he* who forgets *me*—a theme that has cropped up on a number of occasions and is associated with the understanding that as a baby he was allergic to breast milk—that is, that in infancy he rejected his mother? Is it, therefore, his rejection of the breast that must not be acknowledged, but quickly transformed into feeling rejected?

What I said was, "That would put you in a very difficult position." He replied, "Yes, I'd have to back down, even though I knew I was right." He then went on to talk about something that had just happened with his current partner, Jane, who had been abroad and should have called him on her return. Mark was expecting to hear from her earlier than he did—a muddle that was possibly to do with a difference in time zones. Although he was well aware of the potential for confusion around this difference, he went on to ignore this as the likely reason for miscommunication and held on to the injured feeling of being both neglected and culpable. He seemed to be working towards an aggrieved position, for which he appeared to want to enlist my support. The countertransference feeling was, not surprisingly, the opposite, struck as I was by the discrepancies in what he had been saying. This feeling was familiar, and it tended to alert me to an impending cul-de-sac. I wondered why he wanted to take me down this dead end. I turned my attention back to the earlier part of the session, the lightly delivered introductory rebuke for both forgetting and then blaming him, and noted the similarity to what had recently happened with Jane. I remarked on these similarities, adding that both seemed to be related to feelings around separation, or being forgotten. I wondered if there were any further thoughts or feelings connected to this fantasy.

After a few moments, he said that he now wondered whether it was more difficult to believe that I might *remember* him over the break, and that he found this thought more uncomfortable than being forgotten. He then spoke about his fear of becoming too dependent, and the same thing would happen with me as happened in his other relationships: I'd get frustrated and fed up and would want to get rid of him. Perhaps it was simply better to be forgotten, for which he could blame my absent-mindedness, rather than risk (being a) disappointment.

In this exchange he was able to stay with my allusion to the transference relationship with me, openly and in a sustained way. The session continued, recalling earlier themes that related to confusion around being rejected or rejecting, and he began tentatively to wonder how he might contribute to sustaining this particular set of internal relationships. In this way, we felt we were coming to understand not only some of the contents of his internal world, but something of how it may operate.

In presenting part of this session to colleagues discussing once-a-week therapy, it was noted that the session dealt with material in a manner that was indistinguishable from sessions that take place at greater frequency, in terms of unconscious processes, associative material, interpretation of that material along with aspects of the patient's resistance, as understood through my experience of the transference and countertransference. All of which, of course, took place in a regular setting—in other words, the necessary conditions of psychoanalytical psychotherapy. If the theme of the group discussion hadn't been "frequency", the issue may not have arisen.

The question for me is: can this work be done, or done (as) effectively, when the patient attends as infrequently as once a week? Am I still practising psychoanalytic psychotherapy, by which I mean the therapeutic process that results from putting psychoanalytic theory into practice? If not, what am I—and what are others like me—doing? Alongside the innate capacity of the individual patient, is it necessary to evolve a technique—still based on the values, structures, and boundaries of this practice—that is appropriate for this scale of work, which is, after all, an increasing reality for many practitioners? In this chapter, I wish to explore some of the issues related to frequency and to some possible implications for the development of technique in this regard.

Frequency

Freud himself wrote relatively little on the subject of frequency, but where he did, he advocated five to six sessions per week other than for patients who were in the later stages of therapy. In his paper, "On Beginning the Treatment",[1] he writes:

> For slight cases, or the continuation of a treatment which is already well advanced, three days a week will be enough. ... When the hours of work are less frequent, there is a risk of not being able to keep pace with the patient's real life and of the treatment losing contact with the present and being forced into by-paths. [Freud, 1913c, p. 111]

As they stand, these do not seem to me to be compelling arguments either for or against frequency. The phrase "real life" in particular is problematic since it is precisely the reality of the *inner world* that distinguishes this process.

It may, of course, be the case that the more consistent the "dailyness" of contact, the more readily are evoked the conditions of early relationships, and therefore the state of infantile dependency, that give rise to the feelings and associations that provide the material for the work. But even the most rigorous practice provides only a model of attachment and continuity—a metaphor that can do no more than evoke the actual conditions of infancy. How far can this model of dailyness be challenged and still remain effective?

Etchegoyen elaborates on the argument in favour of greater frequency, stating:

> Most analysts think the most convenient rhythm for analysis is five sessions per week.... [This] seems to me the most adequate, because it establishes a substantial period of contact and a clear break at the weekend.... A rhythm as inconsistent and alternating as an analysis every *other* day does not ... enable conflict of contact and separation to arise with sufficient strength. The treatments of one or two sessions per week do not generally constitute a psychoanalytic process ... [but] psychotherapy—that is *dispersion or omission of the transference, manifest or latent reassurance formulated as interpretation, neglect of separation anxiety* ... and so forth. [Etchegoyen, 1991, pp. 512–514; italics added].

The implicit argument here suggests that what is perceived as inadequate analysis of the transference—inattention to separation anxiety, acts of reassurance, and so forth—are *by definition* psychotherapy, whereas their effective counterparts are understood as psychoanalysis. If everything is there *but* the frequency, is it still psychoanalytic psychotherapy, and can once-a-week sessions, under certain conditions, be enough to bring about the "deep-going changes in the mind" that Freud indicates are the hallmark of successful treatment?

Expanding on issues of setting, Merton Gill (1988) argues that "psychoanalytic technique can be used even if the external conditions are not what is considered optimal for an analysis", adding, "I do not accept frequent sessions, the couch, and a patient considered analysable according to the usual definitions to be defining criteria of analysis" (pp. 262–274). He reminds us that "the range of circumstances of therapies which Freud called psychoanalysis varied enormously in terms of overall duration, frequency, and couch or face to face", with the material of several very short-term treatments contributing seminally to both the formulation and communication of psychoanalytic concepts,

and which Freud clearly considered as examples of sound practice. Gill maintains that such practice did not breach Freud's
own theories.

Key concepts

In his *Critical Dictionary of Psychoanalysis* (1968) the late Charles
Rycroft[2] describes "psychoanalysis" as a form of treatment the
"key defining concepts" of which are: (a) *free association*; (b)
interpretation; and (c) *transference*, and which, in practice, consists
in the [psychoanalytically oriented] therapist providing an *environment* that will enable the patient to associate freely, and
then in interpreting those associations, as well as the patient's
resistance to the process, and his feelings and attitude towards
the therapist. According to this minimal definition, then, the
therapist is working with the patient's *unconscious*, his *resistance*
(often his resistance to association), the numerous *defences* employed to sustain that resistance, and the phenomenon and use
of transference. This is similar to the description covered in
Laplanche and Pontalis's *Language of Psychoanalysis* (1973),
which refers directly to Freud's own 1922 encyclopaedia definition. None of these definitions mentions frequency.
    To summarize the Key Concepts, these are:

- a theory that attends to unconscious processes;
- a practice that both elicits and then interprets the patient's
  associations, as well as the resistances and defences thereby
  aroused, particularly as these relate to libidinal wishes;
- the aim (ideal, or often idealized) of resolving the transference within a regular and reliable setting.

Today countertransference would certainly be included in this
very basic list and, given their unique place in both the history
and the ongoing practice of psychotherapy, dreams[3] (Freud,
1905e [1901]). But is this list sufficient for effective practice at
any frequency, and are there implications for modification of
technique?

Free-floating attention

In terms of carrying out this practice, Freud remarks on the analyst's impressive capacity to remember so many of the facts and details pertaining to each individual patient, but he states:

> The technique . . . is a very simple one . . . [I]t rejects the use of any special expedient. . . . It consists simply in not directing one's notice to anything in particular and in maintaining the same 'evenly suspended attention' . . . in the face of all that one hears. [Freud, 1912e, p. 111]

This technique is preferable to a more intentional attitude:

> For as soon as anyone deliberately concentrates his attention . . . he begins to select from the material before him; one point will be fixed in his mind with particular clearness and some other will be correspondingly disregarded, and in making this selection he will be following his expectations or inclinations. [Freud, 1912e, p. 112]

The implication for Freud's recommendation is not that the therapist is *not* selecting, but that the selection is less deliberate and takes place in a different "register" of attention.[4]

At the same time, to be effective, the therapist must also be able to process, link, connect, and—indeed—select, in order to make meaning of the material of the session, and reflect this back to the patient. Writing in 1919, Sándor Ferenczi articulated this apparently complex process in these terms:

> Analytic therapy . . . makes claims on the doctor that seem directly self-contradictory. On the one hand, it requires of him the free play of association and phantasy, the full indulgence of his own unconscious . . . [in order to] grasp intuitively the expressions of the patient's unconscious that are concealed in the manifest material of the manner of speech and behavior. On the other hand, the doctor must subject the material submitted by himself and the patient to a logical scrutiny, and in his dealings and communications may only let himself be guided exclusively by the result of this mental effort. [Ferenczi, 1919, p. 189]

Writing on this subject more recently, C. Brenneis (1994) comments on this duality, stating that

> In large measure psychoanalytic training consists in the development of the rigorous self-discipline necessary for shifting between free-floating intuitive modes of perception and more structured and reflective modes. . . . under ideal conditions psychoanalytic listening develops a rhythmic sequence between a "receiving" and a "restructuring" mode. The former emphasizes subjectivity and has as its goal the translation of words into images; the latter emphasizes conceptual thought and has as its goal symbol formation. [Brenneis, 1994, p. 29]

He refers to Freedman (1983), who positions listening at the heart of the enterprise, stating: "Listening is an effort at the construction of meaning . . . [and] in this sense, the listening process is the *sine qua non* of psychoanalytic treatment." The capacity for such "rhythmic oscillation" between the intuitive and the restructuring functions inherent in analytic listening is, for Freedman, "the essence of the psychoanalytic process itself"—a process that is described as "somewhat unconscious and quite involuntary" (pp. 405–436), very like the listening state aptly captured by Freud's phrase: "evenly suspended attention"—a term to which Brenneis (1994) refers as the "baseline mode" (p. 35) of listening, which is a continually oscillating process and which relies not so much on frequency as on experience (although the two are obviously not contradictory).

Containment

The implication for once-a-week sessions is that by their nature they may feel "compressed", and the tendency in the session may be to "concentrate"—in both senses of the word. In so doing, a sense—or a fantasy—of urgency may be engendered, alongside a corresponding urgency in relation to containment. It may be that this sense of anxiety regarding containment places greater pressure on the therapist to affirm or reassure, or to "round off" the session as an act of holding, but in so doing risk forfeiting the "rhythm" and "oscillation" that enables the process to move forward.

What I am suggesting here is that the containing function of the once-weekly session may be more likely to be established, strengthened, and sustained through adhering to the same processes as are practised in more frequent sessions, by staying in touch with and interpreting unconscious contents as they become available and as they are revealed through transference and countertransference communication. This requires, on the part of the therapist, a careful monitoring of both the processes, as well as of the patient's responses, particularly in relation to what has taken place in the gap between sessions. However, provided these are regular and reliable, a "network" of communication may thus be established that can survive separation because the experience within the session is that the patient has a recognized place within the mind of the therapist—which may, of course, not be at all a comfortable place for many patients, whatever the frequency. As with any patient, the task for the therapist is to acknowledge and interpret within the session the impact of the separation between sessions, but given that the duration of separation in once-a-week work is considerably greater than the instances of contact, this may require an added sensitivity to the patient's anxiety around being "separate" and all that that implies. The tendency of some once-a-week patients to "serialize" the sessions, for example, treating them as instalments, may be an expression of such anxiety concerning the capacity of the therapy—or the therapist—to "hold" them, or indeed their own ability to be held in their absence. Such tactics may serve as an indication of the patient's need to take up the responsibility of sustaining continuity on behalf of the therapy and would need to be acknowledged and addressed.

What I am suggesting, therefore, is that careful technique—regardless of frequency—may enable patients to recognize that they do not have to be *there* to be *held*: a mutual space may be created, made available, and then sustained, even in silence or absence. The counterpart to this recognition that the patient can be held in mind over a period of separation is that the therapist establishes in the patient's unconscious a presence that is equally sustaining in the gap between sessions and a holding structure that can begin to be built. This is obviously not about conscious memory, but about the capacity to feel held from within that enables reverie, connection, and, ultimately, the self-containment necessary to endure separation. The task of the therapist will be to learn from one week to the next, and perhaps over a trial period of time, whether the patient's (and possibly the therapist's) anxiety can been sufficiently contained to be able to continue to work in this way.

Anxieties about frequency make themselves known in a number of ways.

Jackie, for example, a middle-aged journalist, tends to relate to the therapy primarily through dreams, and to other relationships mainly through daydreams. She often fills her once-a-week sessions with accounts of dreams that are not precisely recurrent, but have a very familiar ring to them. Issues around containment became heightened during a break, and upon her return she reported that she'd had many dreams over the holiday, and began to tell me the first that came to mind. *We were together in the consulting-room, and there were only two minutes left to the session. She felt she had much to say, but couldn't—there was not enough time. I became somewhat upset, left her and went into another room to play the piano. She remained on the couch and listened to me playing, thinking that I interpreted the music well.*

She was then reminded of another dream that she'd had over the break. "It's also about you", she said. *She entered the consulting-room, but someone came in and said that I was away. Jackie said she knew that but that she was allowed to come anyway. She got changed into her pyjamas and got into a bed with green sheets, like her own. Again, there was a piano. Then she noticed that another girl was waiting as well, and Jackie realized that she had to go, but she couldn't get the door open.*

An image then came to her from another dream, of *a postcard with an evangelic scene. I was in the background of the image, and there seemed to be something magical about it. Then I disappeared, leaving a slight halo.* After a pause, she said there was still one more dream to tell, only this time I wasn't in it. *She sees a man sucking his penis which is deep in his throat. She wonders how he will get it out. His mother—who is a strong Italian woman—releases it with forceps, like pulling out a baby.*

There was about 15 minutes left to the session. She said that it seemed that although she hadn't been consciously thinking about the sessions over the break, she had the feeling that she'd been dreaming about them the whole time. I suggested that she may have found a way to continue with the sessions during the break, and that now she was bringing to me the self that had been away—thereby closing the gap. However, the dreams seemed to speak of longing, rebuke, and helplessness. They appeared to be suggesting that she never has enough time with me, that I'm impatient with her, that I'd rather be alone in my own mind (play the piano in another room) than be with her, that others take precedence, and that the more she comes to depend on me, the greater the risk that I may disappear. I seem to be tantalizing and elusive. All of this is recognizable from what we know of her internal world. The last dream seemed to suggest a very enclosed, regressed, auto-erotic world, which presents itself as an alternative to the risk of relating to a potentially rejecting, narcissistic, and *absent* object—but it's deadly and solipsistic. In the dream a forceful mother deals with the situation directly, as a gynaecologist extracts a baby who is stuck in the birth canal. This, too, is risky but may be necessary for survival. I also refer to Jackie's tendency to fill the session with dreams, such that—in the 50 minutes we have each week—there is little opportunity to reflect together at length on their meaning, thereby ensuring that I understand how it feels not to have enough time.

This patient might well benefit from increased sessions, but that is not possible at this moment. In her material there are often references to time—as there were in the dreams—and clearly it is important to recognize and acknowledge that the patient may want more than either the therapist is able to give or the patient is able to get.

However, in developing effective once-a-week technique, the therapist may enable an internal sense of continuity to be established through the experience of being held within the mind of the therapist, rather than solely through a more "linear" narrative that may characterize some once-a-week sessions. As long as sessions are regular and reliable, this holding function (ideally) enables the patient both to use the weekly encounter more effectively and to feel connected over the separation. Still, the development of this technique in relation to low-frequency work must make distinct demands on the practitioner and no doubt requires considerable experience, especially in the area of psychoanalytic listening.

Psychoanalytic listening

Recently a number of writers (Baranger, 1993; Brenneis, 1994; Faimberg, 1992; Gill, 1988; Makari & Shapiro, 1993) have been investigating the primarily unconscious communication between patient and therapist, in which the emphasis is on the inversion of values between "noise" and "communication" in psychoanalytic, as opposed to conventional, listening. All of these explorations seem to me to be equally applicable to all psychoanalytically based practice, irrespective of frequency.

Many indirect forms of listening take place within the analytic encounter. Communication may begin with the patient's arrival, prior even to vision or speech. The session itself may begin with a ritual greeting on the part of the patient, with no acknowledgement whatever of the break between sessions, with something thoughtful, or diverting, with hostility, or with silence. What happens next is, I think, often what the patient is waiting for—to hear, or to discover, how or whether he has been held in mind. Some of this process is discussed by Haydée Faimberg (1992) in what she calls "listening to listening". In speaking of what she describes as the "countertransference position", Faimberg writes:

> The first relevant factor is the patient's discourse—not only what he says but also what he does not say—which determines how the analyst listens to him. . . .

This communication is then processed countertransferentially and

> At a first stage, the analyst listens to the patient and chooses either to interpret or to remain silent. At a second stage, he listens to how the patient has himself listened to the interpretation or the silence. This second stage gives retroactive meaning to the first stage and allows the analyst to begin to listen to this barely audible register. Since the patient cannot speak directly about the way he has listened to the interpretations or refer to his unconscious identifications, it is up to the analyst to listen to the way in which these speak. [Faimberg, 1992, p. 545]

She calls this function of the analyst "listening to listening".

The issue for therapists is how this listening influences their judgement in selecting from the many often contradictory messages that are surfacing from the material. If the therapist seems to hear only the narrative, the surface or "manifest content"—and this may be a tendency in once-weekly sessions—then the patient hears this too and may sense the concern that there is insufficient time to hear more deeply. He then understands that he must continue to be responsible for holding himself (in, or over) until the next session, perhaps reinforcing the initial condition of inadequate containment. If however therapists are able to communicate that they have heard and are responsive to the underlying communication, then the patient has the opportunity to internalize this and to experience the sense of continuity and connection from one week, or one session, to the next.

In order to foster this position, which part of the communication in the analytic session do we therefore attend to: what guides our selection?—the words, sentences, or narrative, which surely cannot be ignored, or the underlying, the unspoken, the discrepancies, the *non sequiturs*? The question is why the underlying affect has "selected" this particular mode of communication. I think what we are often inwardly processing is the material that *links* these layers, and this is achieved through the sort of layered listening that is described above. As Makari and Shapiro (1993) phrase it: "Unconscious communication is the story that emerges again and again despite the story-teller; paradoxically, it is also the tale the storyteller validates" (p. 1005).

A clinical example that explores some of these listening-related concerns is illustrated by a session in which the patient related a dream, and offered her own interpretation, which was, I believe, based on the work that had been taking place in the once-weekly sessions over a period of some months, and in particular the way in which the patient felt she was being heard.

> Mary, a woman in her mid–30s, comes from a very abused background. She had been accustomed to both thinking of herself and describing herself as "bubbly" as well as "open and honest", but recently she had begun to wonder about the reality of her apparent candour, particularly in relation to her very troubled background. She had begun to question her motives with regard to her openness and became uncomfortable about the potential for manipulating people with her frankness about her early life. The implication was that she was also not altogether as "honest" as she believed herself to be, and this realization both surprised and discomfited her. Mary "knew" that her family history and experience were appalling, but she was accustomed to speaking about it with a detachment that was both disarming and disconcerting. I, however, had become aware of feelings in myself of outrage, sadness, and futility—feelings that informed my comments during the sessions prior to the dream.
>
> Mary began the session immediately describing her dream, in which *she was visiting the optician, a woman, who was saying to her that to examine her properly, she, Mary, had to cover one eye with her hand, so that the optician might test the other eye. Mary protested that this was unnecessary, since she knew quite well what*

she needed in the way of glasses, and such a thorough examination in her case was a waste of time. The optician, however, repeated that this was the only way in which to make a proper examination. Mary again protested, but the optician insisted on carrying out the procedure correctly. Mary eventually agreed to do this, only to discover that she was in fact blind in the other eye.

Mary was sure that I was the optician and that the dream was referring to our recent sessions, in which she felt she'd been coming to the idea that her apparent candour was a camouflage. She felt that she'd been "turning a blind eye"— or that she really hadn't wanted to acknowledge the emotional impact of what had happened to her. Recently, she felt that I'd been turning my attention more to what hadn't been said than what had been—like the optician in the dream— and indicating that something important (in this case, her emotional connection to her experience) was being habitually disavowed. Mary did almost all of the work in this session, and she felt clear about the dream referring to our sessions and to her own history of denial, which was becoming unavoidably clear through the therapy. This was in no way about recovered memory: the material had always been available to her and was even well documented. But the feelings had long been split off and had only begun to return during the therapy. Of course, it is almost certainly the case that further sessions in the week would have elicited more material and perhaps deepened and consolidated the experience. Nonetheless, I believe that the work that was done included both transference and countertransference components, attention to attachment, and feelings around separation, and that the patient had felt sufficiently well held to be able to internalize and process the material from earlier sessions in such a way as to feel internally connected to the therapy over the period of separation. This may not, of course, be true of all patients.

It is almost certainly the case that a sense of the direction of the therapy, what is being resisted or avoided, what is being emphasized and repeated, may be more apparent when the patient is seen more frequently. Furthermore, the character of once-a-week work may tend to reinforce the patient/therapist relationship over and above the patient–internal object relationship, which may, in turn, affect the internally transformative impact of the work. All of these considerations are aspects of once-a-week listening and interpretation that demand specific attention and supervision.

Conclusion

Certain concepts are common to all psychoanalytically based therapy, regardless of frequency: these include the prioritization of unconscious processes, which are gradually understood through the patient's speech, silences, associations, and responses; the specific interactivity between patient and therapist as understood through the patient's transference and the therapist's countertransference, which—alongside other material—the therapist endeavours to interpret.

The central activity of the therapist is a sensitized form of listening—a key tool, regardless of frequency, but especially important in once-a-week work as the manner of listening itself, which oscillates between intuitive modes on the one hand and restructuring modes on the other, provides an experience of containment for the patient. This, in turn, enables an environment that is both adaptive and rigorous and may serve to sustain a sense of containment over longer periods of separation. This experience may help the patient to feel held, and—perhaps more significantly—"holdable", over the separation from one week to the next.

This is not an argument promoting once-weekly work but—recognizing that this is an increasing reality—more a consideration of "best practice", as the tendency in less frequent work may be towards working less deeply for fear of leaving the patient feeling exposed and uncontained at the end of each session. This chapter is offered as a contribution to fuller thought and discussion on this developing practice.

Notes

1. One of five papers on technique written between 1912 and 1915.
2. I'm using the terms "psychoanalyst" and "psychotherapist" here with reference to Rycroft's description of a "psychoanalytically oriented psychotherapist").
3. ". . . a thorough investigation of the problems of dreams is an indispensable prerequisite for any comprehension of the mental processes in hysteria and the other psychoneuroses, and . . . no one who wishes to shirk that preparatory labour has the smallest prospect of advancing even a few steps into this region of knowledge" (Freud, 1905e [1901], p. 11).
4. Another of the five papers on technique written between 1912 and 1915.

CHAPTER FOUR

Has anyone seen the baby?
Analytic psychotherapy
with mothers who are postnatally
depressed and their babies

Johanna Roeber

In my work in a NHS psychotherapeutic day clinic I see women who have suffered serious trauma as children. That trauma overshadows their whole life. They know something is very wrong, but they don't know what it is. All around them are other women who seem happy with their babies; they think that perhaps having a baby will make them also happy, and when that does not happen, that disturbs them even more, and after the birth they become depressed. When they come into treatment, they bring their babies with them, and so I have both the mother's internal baby and the real baby in the consulting-room. The insecure patterns of relating that the mother has suffered are vividly demonstrated in her interaction with her child. Before my eyes I see the damage the mother has suffered being handed on to the next generation.

Analytic psychotherapy with a postnatally depressed mother who brings her infant to all of her sessions poses many questions. Whom is the therapist to see as the patient: the mother, the baby, or the relationship between the two? Bertrand Cramer (1993) found that there is a "relationship disorder" between mother and infant in the clinical condition called postpartum depression. Maintaining the focus of intervention exclusively on the mother seems artificial, particularly when there is a baby playing an active non-verbal part in the consulting-room and often showing signs of disturbance as well. As Paul Barrows (2000) points out, a mother's postnatal depression creates an urgent need to address the problematic parent–infant relationship rather than focus on an individual in the dyad. And what about the baby's father? His childhood experiences and his relationship with mother and baby have been shown to be highly influential when thinking about maternal depression and infant disturbances in the postpartum period (Daws, 1989). Trying to address these different demands for treatment is perplexing.

Joan Raphael-Leff (1991) has pointed out that analytical psychotherapy invites regression in the mother as she makes links with memories of her infant experience of parents, siblings, and other important figures from her past. A mother brings to each pregnancy a powerful cocktail of projections that the baby stimulates. Where the mother has suffered difficulties in childhood, the birth of a baby can evoke in her conflicts that prompt her to re-enact with her baby the unremembered "ghosts in the nursery" (Fraiberg, Adelson, & Shapiro, 1975), with disastrous results. Although analytic psychotherapy does encourage regression, it also gives form and meaning to the distortions that the baby carries in the mother's mind. Raphael-Leff also emphasizes that the mother's healthy adult resources need to be recognized and activated to strengthen the positive aspects of her relationship with the baby. With this in mind, and because the baby is present, I felt that analytic psychotherapy alone might be insufficient.

For the baby, verbal interpretations—the "talking cure" approach of psychotherapy—run the risk of missing the point. The baby is in a non-verbal stage that Winnicott (1960) describes as "psyche indwelling in the soma". Normal communication occurs through sounds, smell, body movements and gestures, facial expression, and gaze. The baby is an active instigator in the relationship with his mother and his environment, as Daniel Stern's (1985) work has shown. Here is a potential ally in the clinical endeavour if his contribution is noticed and encouraged. A baby is highly sensitive to the people around him, and how he behaves in the consulting-room indicates the current state of his relationship with his mother. As soon as the mother's therapy begins, I try to observe the baby. What the baby communicates to me, how he does it, and at what point is always relevant and part of my thinking about the mother's session. My counter-transference is also an essential tool.

Bearing in mind the mother's need for verbal communication and the baby's need for non-verbal communication, I found that my approach began to differ from the classical psychoanalytic model. There is evidence that combining psychotherapy for the mother with a non-verbal therapy such as dance therapy (Coulter & Loughlin, 1999) for mother and infant addresses the complexity of need. In this Australian project mother-and-baby had individual psychotherapy and then both participated in a group dance therapy programme over 12 weeks. This approach, and other short-term therapies with mothers and babies (Cramer, 1997), is based on the premise that the mother and baby interaction not only demonstrates the pathology of the relationship but can also be a vehicle for change. However, where the mother's own pathology is highly disturbed, approaching the mother–infant relationship directly often provokes too much anxiety in the mother. Moreover, I have noticed that severely disturbed mothers cannot use group activities until they have had some individual psychotherapy to enable them to feel less paranoid and anxious.

In an ideal world it is helpful to meet both parents with the baby when treating maternal disturbances in the postnatal period. It has been shown that where there is good social support, the mother's depression is lessened (Brown & Harris, 1978). Helping a father to understand the difficulties in the family so that he can support the mother–infant relationship is sensible. However, often the father has himself had a traumatic childhood that can be part of the problem. How to get reluctant fathers involved in treatment is beyond the scope of this chapter. In our clinic once contact has been made, a father might be offered treatment for himself, or family meetings, whichever seems appropriate. It is interesting that Dilys Daws (1989), in her work with sleepless infants, sees parents and mothers with babies and finds that both combinations work well.

Many of my patients who have suffered early traumas find that when they give birth, internal psychic tensions increase to an unbearable pitch. A healthy part of them is mobilized to seek help. Meanwhile they care for the baby physically, although this arouses emotions of envy and hatred in mothers who feel so deprived of care and attention themselves. Violent phantasies and impulses leave the mother feeling a social outcast. They often fear that they have harmed the baby irrevocably, and guilt is a major source of maternal suffering. Paradoxically, it is the birth of the baby that precipitates the mother's breakdown and the baby who mobilizes the help that is a potential for change.

So what do I do? As soon as I meet the mother and her baby, I want to make contact with them both. However, if the mother is very disturbed herself, it is vital that she feel contained, and so I concentrate my attention on her. Naturally I observe the baby and what happens between him and his mother. It is important to notice what happens between me and the baby, and I try to remember when any interaction takes place in the session to think about it later. I am also curious about how the mother reacts to my interest in her baby. For the very deprived mothers I see, it often feels unbearable to have to share me with the baby. I make it clear to the mother that her baby is important to me and that I will protect him if necessary. A mother who fears harming her child is also anxious about losing her child if she reveals herself to me. It takes courage to seek treatment and to persist against inner persecution, and this needs to be acknowledged. However, for many of the mothers who are referred to the clinic, issues of child protection have to be kept in mind. I have continuously to balance the mother's need for me to process her evacuated distress and respond to her infantile anxiety—as Bion (1962a) described it—and the baby's need to be protected in the real world.

As soon as treatment begins, the mother's internal, highly deprived baby becomes very demanding. The transference develops rapidly and is very intense. Because there is a mother and a baby in the room, my feelings in the countertransference have a particular quality. I am struck by my overreaction and by how much I want to be helpful (Segal, 1981). I often have a sense of disappointment in myself where I feel in the position of a bewildered, helpless child weighed down by projections coming from a distraught but unavailable mother. At times I feel under murderous attack from a patient who wishes to annihilate me but who clings to me in fear of her own annihilation. Both mother and baby arouse intense emotions in me that I struggle to understand; later in the therapy I can use these to inform a mother. Dilys Daws expressed the challenges of the countertransference well when she wrote:

> A worker offering receptivity will equally be assailed by emotions coming from both baby and mother ranging from voracious greed to an inability to take in what is offered. Empathy with mother and baby can be exhausting and draining as though one *is a* demanding perplexed baby, or a mother who has no resources left, or exhilarated as though one is an ideal mother/grand-mother who always has more to give. [Daws, 1993, p. 75]

During a session I try to hold three generations—grandmother, mother, and baby—in my mind. I also try to hold an awareness of fatherliness for each generation, because so often fathers have been absent or disruptive. I am available to the mother—as Bion (1962a) described it—as the ". . . receptor organ for the infant's harvest of self-sensation gained by its conscious." And I am available to the baby as an observer who is trying to understand.

The therapeutic alliance is working well when the mother begins to develop a narrative of her own childhood experiences of anxiety and suffering with the appropriate feelings. These feelings that have been split off are intensely painful and disruptive when they emerge into consciousness. When the confusion between the past and the present becomes a little more manageable, I am alert to the liberation of the healthy part of the mother that will allow me to include the baby—and his communications—in our work. When she feels sufficiently alive and contained in my mind, the mother is able to allow her relationship with her baby a separate place in our thinking. Then we can have a verbal maternal "reverie" about the baby. This process is completely bewildering to the mother at first, and if my timing is wrong, it makes her feel even more anxious and persecuted. I start with simple observations, noting and reflecting on any changes in the baby's smell, in his gestures and movements, or in the sounds he makes. I wonder aloud about what the baby is trying to communicate. How does he show pleasure and pain? How is he feeling at a given moment? I openly appreciate any insight or sensitive observation the mother makes, or any comfortable exchange between her and her baby. Gradually the mother, and often the baby, lead the way. The mother's confidence in her resources in relation to her baby increases, and she feels less persecuted about her failures. The movement "in" and "out" of psychotherapy's classical format does create problems, and sometimes the boundaries are breached. There are inevitable consequences to altering my technique, which include the risk of enactment, but usually the patient and I do recover, and over time, the therapeutic benefit is considerable for both mother and child.

Jane and her baby

Jane said that her mother had "adored" her from birth. As a baby, she had been carried about by her mother, who used her as a human shield against a violent, alcoholic husband. Jane talks about this coldly and with composure. Her lack of affect and inability to manage strong feelings has been the pattern of her life ever since. She was a year old when her brother was born and she lost her place in mother's arms.

Being used by mother as a shield and then dropped so traumatically resulted in her turning to father and identifying with him. She developed a false self, and, as the "good little girl", Jane suppressed her real feelings for the sake of a fragile sense of control. As she said later in her therapy: "In my house there was so much shit and violence flying about there was no room for me, or my feelings. Mum and Dad fought blue murder and then pretended nothing had happened." Jane's statement could also be seen as an accurate description of her inner world. Her objects are engaged in excited and terrifying violence, and so she cuts off, she deadens her feelings in order to survive. As an adult the excited violence of her internal world is translated into an attraction to sex with violent men.

Jane is a single parent by design. She has no contact with the father of her baby. She had the idea that getting pregnant would mean that she would discover good feelings in herself. Unconsciously she longed for a baby who would love—and stay with—the unlovable part of herself. But when the baby was born after a traumatic labour, she found she had no feelings at all.

Jane wanted to change a profoundly stuck part of herself. Strong emotions terrified her, and she had always dealt with them by cutting herself off. But a baby has strong feelings and stirs strong feelings because of its vulnerability and neediness. A baby cannot wait and so easily becomes a persecuting object for the mother. Rather than increasing the mother's sense of narcissistic well-being, the baby is felt to be attacking and undermining her fragile sense of self. The baby becomes a part-object in the mother's mind—a container of unwanted and terrifying aspects of the self representation that need to be eliminated (Perelberg, 1999). When my patient could no longer cope by cutting off her feelings, she became highly disturbed. The baby had failed her, as had everyone else. When she met me, she told me that my job was to put things right.

Clinical work

During the initial stages of our work each session begins in the same way: Jane is always early. However, when I look into the waiting-room, I can't see her, and I have to peer round the corner to discover her and her baby Alex, asleep in the pushchair. I say "Hello", but Jane seems lost in her own thoughts. She gives me a brief smile but then says in a dead voice, "I don't know what to do." Waving at the baby, she adds wildly, "I don't want this with me." She points at the pushchair, but I know she's also referring to the baby. In the clinic the arrangement is for pushchairs to be left with the receptionist, but each time Jane seems at a loss and waits for me to suggest it. Reluctantly, Jane lifts the sleeping baby, I wheel the pushchair into the office and carry the baby's bag, and we process upstairs to my room. At the start of every session we perform the same ritual of my having to "locate" her and then suggest a place for the pushchair. I think this indicates how unsure she is that her object will want to retrieve her and find a way to stay with her. But it also shows her passivity and sadism towards the mother–baby couple. When I dispose of the pushchair, Jane feels I become sadistic because I force her into bodily contact with her baby. This increases her anxiety and therefore her aggression (Freud, 1926d [1925]). Once inside the room, Jane plonks the sleeping baby on the floor between us, but so that he will see me if he wakes. She is letting me know that she will not be mother. She stares silently out the window, and I acknowledge her difficulty in meeting me again and having to share me with her baby. She ignores me, but after a while she catches my eye and snaps angrily: " I can't think with him in here, I have nothing to say, my mind's a blank."

I am familiar with Jane's sessions beginning in this way, and I have come to understand that she is describing her desperation when she is forced to respond to her baby's needs and carry him upstairs. She feels envious of Alex's needs being met when she herself feels so neglected. Mother and baby together evoke her traumatic memories of being carried and then dropped in favour of her younger brother. At these moments in the transference I become the dangerous sibling that has to be killed if she is to preserve her sense of self. My attempts to make contact are seen as proof of guilt. At these moments Jane's defences are in danger of being breached: she fears regression to a helpless state of "non-existence" (Mitchell, 2000).

Feeling excluded and under attack, I look towards the baby (perhaps for reassurance?), who suddenly wriggles and gurgles. Internally I wonder about his experience, while processing the material between his mother and myself. Jane, who is ever watchful of shifts in my attention, looks at her baby as well.

Then she turns away, muttering that she needs a cigarette. I remark that maybe she felt left out when I looked at Alex and he "said" something. Because Jane consciously denies that Alex has any feelings, she looks sulky and says: "I don't understand you. Anyway, he didn't *say* anything, he's just a baby." Jane speaks in a dismissive tone of voice, which tells me that after her smile of fruitful contact when she felt "found" in the waiting-room, she is now feeling displaced and therefore murderous. She dismisses me because she fears that access to her state of mind will lead to a loss of control, and so she rejects the despised victim and becomes the triumphant aggressor. As Estela Welldon (1988) says: "From being the victim, such people become the victimizers. In their actions they are the perpetrators of the victimization and humiliation previously inflicted upon them" (p. 9). Jane drops me, as she dropped the baby and as she felt she was dropped by her mother. She shows me that any attempt I make to contact her will be perceived as weak, in comparison with her cruel satisfaction derived from the way she cuts me off. In her mind I become a mixture of the hated rival and the denigrated maternal object. Having triumphed over me, she feels safe temporarily. The baby's response to my glance means that he has separated himself from her and has bestowed his "gift" of a gurgle on me. She feels unloved and excluded from this warm exchange. She has to cut off from us both.

This may be seen as pretty ordinary borderline material—the stuff of all our work. Yet Jane's dilemma has a particularly destructive quality now she is a mother. The baby, an object of manic reparation whose conception was part of an idealized phantasy, has in reality brought the threat of breakdown by exposing Jane's original trauma and fragile defences.

Jane's wish to experience loving feelings towards her baby (the conscious reason for getting pregnant) has had the reverse effect by increasing her fear of losing control of the sadistic rage that erupts when she becomes aware of intense emotion. In Jane's mind the baby has failed her, and he inevitably becomes a bad object that threatens her stability. Her need to control and deaden her feelings escalates. Her transference to me is activated around feeling projectively identified with her object in a narcissistic dyad. Any separation from me arouses her anxiety of being abandoned. Being alone arouses her terror of the victim state of mind, and all her defences are activated to protect her from disintegration. Awareness of the baby as a separate person transforms him into a dangerous rival or a disappointing maternal object. So she strips him of meaning, and he becomes something to be disposed of—like the pushchair. Any attempt on my part to interpret her anxiety about separation or the needy feelings aroused by our coming together is ridiculed. Her needy part is not allowed to have life—any more than the baby is. She signals to me that she is not going to be penetrated by my ideas, but she is ready to allow me to go on longing for contact. However, she will only allow contact with the harsh, cruel part of her that she admires. When she stares out of the window I feel that she becomes unreachable, identified with father's sadistic phallus, which obliterates motherliness.

Continuation

For the first five months of our work I could not begin a "reverie" about her baby with Jane. She struggled with the rage and anger that accompanies the intense grief of a child who has been traumatized, both by a violent rupture when her mother dropped her and from the prolonged absence of affective interaction. She was not able to access her grief and was strongly identified with the sadistic, but unavailable father. She tried to maintain her habitual non-feeling state of mind, but by telling me odd fragments about her childhood she discovered feelings in a "me" trying to make sense of her past. Occasionally her own emotions formed around those memories. This surprised and dismayed her. Jane began to express aggression and frustration towards me—and towards Alex—because she perceived that her loss of control was linked to something we "did" to her. She desperately wanted to stay the "good little girl" without feelings that she had always tried to be. She complained that I didn't give her the exclusively loving feeling she longed for. Any affect stimulated aggression. She felt in danger of disintegrating. She could not acknowledge her emotions about me and ridiculed my efforts to make links with her past conviction that a mother who loved her as the "good" little girl would drop her if she were anything else. There followed a period of anxious stagnation because I felt constrained. If she accessed more of her feelings, there was a risk that she would lose control and attack either me in the session or the baby outside.

After a holiday break when contact has been re-established there was a change. With no affect, looking away from me as usual, Jane told me a dream. *She is in a train with lots of compartments, but it goes too fast to see anything outside. She knows that her mouth is full of shit and she wants to spit it out. Finally she finds a wash-basin and spits the shit out, but it won't go down the plughole, it keeps bubbling back, it's revolting. Then she sees her mother and father holding a dead little girl with blond hair. They are carefully washing the child's hair, and Jane knows that they will cut it off later and sell it. She feels "so what", but she thinks that her hair used to be longer.*

Jane associates to seeing a television film about the Nazis cutting off Jewish prisoners' hair. She tells me that at the time she had no feelings and had thought: "Oh, yes, they did that." There was a silence. She said she felt bad talking about the dream, and she hoped that by telling me she would feel better. I said that she wondered whether I could feel something about her fear that she might be exploited by me, as the little girl was in her dream. She said that the bad part of the dream was the shit in her mouth . . . it was disgusting. I said that the dream was telling us about feeling stuck and not able to get out. But maybe she felt she could be a "shitty" little girl with me and spit out bad things, and I was like the basin that could hold painful things so she might feel better. She said nothing. After a while she said that she knew that I remembered things, and she wished she hadn't told me things about her parents—she wouldn't allow me to think badly of them. Angrily she refused to say more about the dream but told me that when she was little, she was always the good little girl who never complained. I said that when she was little she had no way of thinking about frightening events and feelings because she feared losing her parents whom she needed, so she cut off her feelings instead. There was a silence. Then she said that now she thought about it with me, the film about the Jews was terribly sad.

Jane's dream represented a slight shift in her willingness to trust me. There was sadism and perversion in the dream of the spurious care of the dead child, and the casual link Jane made between herself and the girl in her dream was chilling. However, there was a move to use me like the basin in her dream to spit out the "shit-terror" inside her as I attempted to contain the "nameless dread" of her dreams and phantasies. Gradually, by observing that I was not overwhelmed by her and could still try to think with her, she allowed conflicting feelings to be talked about. Good and bad feelings began to be differentiated. I noticed that she occasionally looked at me (instead of out the window) when I spoke to her about her feelings. I felt moved by her gaze and noticed that my responses became freer and varied. Instead of feeling defensive, I felt more at ease with my feelings about her. Her guilt about cutting off from Alex and her fear of repeating her childhood trauma with her son could be talked about. However, her progress was infinitely slow because of her deeply entrenched defences. Her fear that feelings might lead to uncontrollable anger and murderous rage was taken seriously by us both.

Although Jane's progress in deciphering her feelings and learning to manage them was painfully slow, Alex was growing fast. The need to treat the infant–parent relationship was urgent. As Juliet Hopkins (1992) pointed out: ". . . symptoms in the infant can best be treated by treating the infant–parent relationship, rather than by treating either the infant or parent separately" (p. 7).

Gradually Jane trusted me enough, and our "reverie" about Alex became a regular part of each session. I wanted to be careful not to increase her guilt about her lack of good feelings for her baby. Jane rarely held him or allowed him eye contact, and it did not occur to her to talk to him. I was alarmed by his passivity and pained for him in his isolation. He seemed to have given up trying to reach his mother. He was often "busy" with objects in the corner of the room. His withdrawn behaviour was a symptom of the lack of a relationship between himself and his mother. As time went by, he would catch my eye when I spoke about him or to him, and later he began to crawl to me and touch me. Jane began to feel less persecuted by Alex when she repeatedly experienced that she could recover my attention after I spoke to him or about him. Gradually, as Jane voiced her anger and hatred of her son (an intensely painful experience), she found that paradoxically she could also feel some positive feelings for him as well. Alex made more noises and seemed more demanding, and I could openly appreciate their efforts to make contact with each other. In the session I began to feel slightly encouraged.

In the run-up to a break Alex was suddenly absent. I felt increasingly alarmed by Jane's reports about him. I heard that her father was looking after Alex on a regular basis to give her "a break". Jane justified her cutting off from her son by saying that her father was depressed and "needed to see the baby". Coldly she described how her father encouraged Alex's tears at parting but then called him a "sissy cry-baby". Jane's father also demanded a show of affection from Alex but then suddenly shouted at the baby to "go away". She recalled without emotion that her father had behaved in a similar way towards her when she was a child. Although we discussed what was happening, it was impossible for her to empathize with Alex or to question her sadism in allowing her father to exploit her son's feelings. Her baby, who so often stood for the hated sibling rival, was being tormented for his need for affection, as Jane had been herself. It felt safer to be identified with an unavailable mother so that all needy feelings disappeared. My transference interpretations were rejected. I tried to explore her feelings of being cruelly used by my comings and goings. I suggested that Alex stood for the baby that was cruelly punished for his neediness so she could feel like the abandoning mother. I got nowhere. Her disengagement from me increased if I wondered about Alex's feelings, which she described dismissively as his "tantrums". Her need to occupy a unique place in my mind was clear and acknowledged by me as valid, but my anxiety about the real baby in the real world was becoming unbearable. In the countertransference I felt that I was being invited in a perverse way to join a sadistic "gang" (Rosenfeld, 1971) that observed a baby's pain but did nothing to alleviate it.

Although Jane seemed determined to ignore my concerns about Alex, she mentioned that she'd noticed in the park that other babies cuddled and played with their mothers. She voiced some concern about Alex's reluctance to be held and wanted what she called "advice" from someone who "specialized in children". Because of my anxiety about Alex, I quickly agreed to her consulting a colleague in the clinic about her son's development with a view to having some "play therapy" for herself with Alex. My hope was that Jane (and Alex) could find some practical support in this kind of treatment. Used appropriately, with regular meetings between practitioners, it can be containing for everyone.

I was relieved when Jane and Alex began seeing the play therapist once a week. Jane seemed to be coping with the practical approach with another practitioner, and I hoped that the progress we had made would enable her to accept some help. I left for my break feeling relieved. When I returned, Jane seemed to be doing well. Some weeks later the play therapist suggested making a video of Alex and Jane interacting. Afterwards they looked at it and discussed it. Jane asked if there was a problem, and the therapist replied: "Yes, I can see problems that you should attend to." Jane reacted angrily, demanding another opinion. Feeling intensely persecuted, Jane left the clinic in a rage. After this meeting there was a weekend gap before she saw me again. Jane became extremely anxious and suicidal. She was terrified of being alone with Alex. She put the baby in the pushchair and walked the streets for hours. Eventually she rang the clinic and asked to speak to me and was told I wasn't there. Terrified of her own destructiveness, she rang her mother and asked for help—something she never did. Mother, who is remarried and lives outside London, came and took over the care of the baby.

Jane came to her next session almost speechless with rage, then she erupted. She was furious with everyone—particularly with the play therapist, who had "seen" bad things and told her to put them right. She felt exposed and accused of being a "bad" mother; she refused to go back. The tenuous link with Alex was broken, and she couldn't stand being with him. Things had got worse, not better. All these months and there was no change; she still had no love for Alex, I was useless. Mother didn't understand anything and had already gone home, and now what was she supposed to do with Alex? She was particularly enraged with me because I hadn't been there when she rang the clinic— everyone had let her down. My noting the difference between her fantasy of her ever-abandoning internal objects and the reality of her mother's response to her appeal for help was dismissed.

As she talked, she became angrier and angrier with me. I realized that we had re-enacted her early trauma. She felt that I as mother had dropped her, and she had felt sadistically attacked by the male play therapist as father. Feeling abandoned by me and criticized by the parental play therapist left her at the mercy of violent and sadistic impulses that threatened her equilibrium. She felt flooded with murderous rage towards her baby, who represented the sibling that had been the original threat. I noticed that Alex was abnormally still. Jane kept glancing at him and said she didn't want him to see how upset she was. I said perhaps she wanted to think that Alex didn't know that she was feeling powerful emotions—feeling very angry with me for not being there when she needed me to think together with her about what had happened. Jane said she hated that sugary tone in my voice—she didn't need anyone. Her mother always told her not to show feelings or talk about bad things to strangers. I said that maybe Alex felt like a disapproving mother at this moment, and I was like a stranger whom she didn't feel able to trust. She said that she knew that I thought showing feelings was OK, but she knew differently, and she wasn't going to let Alex see her upset. I said maybe she wanted to protect Alex from being scared of an angry adult who might lose control. She shrugged: yes, she was scared of losing her rag.

I said that "losing her rag" was to play down how angry and hurt she felt with me and with Alex at times, and how hard it was to know how to express her feelings safely to me and to him.

Suddenly she looked directly at me (a furious glare) and agreed. What could she do with all this rage? It was like a burning ball inside her chest, about to explode. I said that we could talk about how she could understand her anger productively and not feel overwhelmed by it. She was silent and turned away to stare out the window. I felt uneasy; I was losing contact with her. She said she wasn't sure that she would be able to come back to see me again because she felt too angry. I said that she was showing me how she had to cut off because she felt so disappointed and let down by me. With a sneer in her voice she said she didn't expect anything from me—after all, it was only a job to me. I said that having been let down by not finding me when she felt so anxious and needed me, it was hard for her to trust me with the next step of finding ways to express her feelings safely. At this point Alex began to whimper. Jane swept him up and sat him on her knees; facing me, held stiffly away from her body, she bounced him up and down. "Stop crying, Alex," she said, "this is not helpful, it's my turn now."

We sat silently together. I felt guilty that because of my anxiety before the break I had failed her by letting her go to the play therapist too soon. Into my mind came an image of Jane being carried—clinging—to her mother but feeling used and unable to make a real contact. I said that it must be hard for her to feel so cut off from me now she had found me. She stopped jiggling the baby and looked disdainful. "I never think about you at all. My father asked what my shrink looked like, and I couldn't tell him anything about you." At that moment I saw that having a denigrating father in her mind eliminated her need for closeness with mother.

Feeling that she had controlled me, Jane said she had a dream to tell me. She laughed and said she was sure I would be pleased, as it was about me. I braced myself, feeling the sadism in her laughter. In the dream *she wants to tell me something important, but there are lots of people around, and she can't get near me.* She laughed again and said how silly dreams are. Then the night before coming to see me she had another dream. This time she *is in a house with lots of rooms, and she goes into one and sees Alex hanging by his dungarees from a pole. She wonders if he is dead, but he isn't.* She fell silent and stared away into the distance. After a pause I ventured a simple comment about the dream telling us something about how hard she found it to get near me and to get my full attention. The silence got heavier, and in a rather tight voice she said: "I was called a bean-pole when I was little, I was weedy and skinny."

In this moment of tension I felt a wave of sadness coming from her. Alex started to cry, twisting himself around to look at his mother. Saying nothing, Jane quickly took out a bottle of milk and stuck it into his mouth where he was sitting whimpering, still unable to see her.

To draw attention to Jane's feelings, to see something inside her, was risky. She thought all feelings were dangerous because they led to loss of control. Any slight shift towards vulnerability stimulated her aggression. In our sessions her unconscious invitation to me was to join her in triumphing over neediness. At these moments I often felt paralysed and unable to speak, fearful that anything I said would provoke more sadism. I felt that her dream was extremely painful but once again she had cut herself off from all feelings. I commented on the house of many rooms that maybe stood for the empty clinic where she lost contact with me at the weekend, and where she and her baby-self are left hanging alone, almost dead. I said she might also be expressing a fear that her baby was at risk near her. Jane ignored me, and I felt helpless and inadequate.

Being part of this sad picture of the wriggling baby being fed from behind with little contact with his mother, I felt a wave of guilt that I had failed to help them. Still sensing her sadness and hearing Alex's searching cry, I said that it seemed to me that she felt that maybe Alex was trying to reach her to comfort her and needed some comfort for himself. There was a sad pause. Then in a subdued tone of voice Jane said that she never knew if she got it right—he never wanted to be held like she'd seen other mothers cuddling their babies, she felt sure that he knew that she didn't love him properly. I said that maybe her guilt kept them apart because she couldn't feel that what she had to offer was good for Alex. Jane said nothing. I asked whether she ever thought of holding him closer when she gave him his bottle. "Not now he can sit up", she replied brusquely. Responding to my earlier feeling of a sad child not knowing how to contact mother, I said that we all needed cuddles from time to time. She said her mother was always telling her to force him and then he'd learn to like it, but she didn't want to force him, it seemed wrong. I said she was trying to respect his need to come to her. Jane said, "Ummm", and we fell silent. Meanwhile I had noticed that Alex had stopped whimpering and was closing his eyes as he sucked, perhaps because we were speaking quietly and the atmosphere in the room had calmed down. I said I wondered if she might feel that Alex was ready for a cuddle now. Jane kept looking at me, and I felt that I was holding her in my gaze. She slowly moved the baby closer to her body, until he was leaning against her. Alex relaxed and continued to take his bottle. We three sat quietly together, and I said how comfortable she had made him feel. I was tempted to comment further but stopped myself, feeling that Jane would easily feel "forced". Soon it was time to end the session. Jane packed up Alex's things and said in a clipped voice, "Next week I'll ask you about weaning if you like." I said that she felt unsure if I could think about her needs and at times think about Alex and her together and still want to go on "feeding" her. As she went through the door, she said: "I can never remember what we've talked about here, I should bring a notebook." Jane felt rejected by my ending the session, so she wiped out her feelings about me to regain control. But she was making a bridge to our next meeting that was hopeful.

Jane was able to continue her therapy with me, but we understood that it had been too soon for her to feel concern about a baby at risk from an absent mother. My encouragement to go to the play therapist was felt to be for my benefit or Alex's, and Jane felt rejected and displaced by a younger baby's needs. Persecutory anxiety was too strong, and in her internal world a vulnerable baby aroused murderous rage in her. Jane did continue her treatment, and I was attacked as the neglecting mother and the absent psychotherapist. There was a development in that she was able to get angry and we both survived. For a long time her outbursts were sad and confused, but if I made any comment about her disappointment, she would strongly deny her feelings. I realized that her work was to verbalize her feelings. Mine was to listen and try to understand and take some responsibility for having inevitably failed her while not retaliating or collapsing.

> . . . I help her because I fail her and am not ashamed by her accusations but accept her anger as right and just. And what is even more important for her is that I accept my failures and am not devalued in my eyes by them. [Masud Khan, 1974, p. 277]

Once Jane's feelings were acceptable, we could think about how she could mobilize her own resourcefulness. In the transference I had to live alongside her with the feelings of hurt and rejection and progress slowly with her working through her grief and the destruction of her phantasy of an ideal therapist who would find her a magic solution. Over time I felt that we began to "play" in the sense that Winnicott (1964) described with children who "work off hate and aggression in play as if aggression were some bad substance that could be got rid of" (p. 234).

I had to tolerate Jane's attacks while protecting myself and the part of herself that increasingly wanted the object to survive. Meanwhile I kept Alex alive in my mind—and in the room by wondering aloud about him to Jane (and to himself). In the real world I continued to feel acutely anxious about mother and child. However, since she had seen the play therapist, we could acknowledge Alex's needs and her feeling of failure more openly, and we began to build on her moments of real contact with Alex. My habit of thinking about him became reassuring to Jane, even though she was very sad and jealous that nobody had thought about her when she was a baby.

Jane needed to find herself in my mind, to feel contained and alive, and only then could she allow Alex to become part of our thinking. This process of giving birth to the baby in the mother's mind normally takes place during pregnancy and then consolidates after the birth. In a good-enough mother's mind she "gives birth" to her baby each time they meet. In this way, as Kenneth Wright (1991) describes it, the baby builds up an image of an alive self from seeing himself reflected lovingly in the mother's eyes. But Jane had experienced Alex as an intruder who had to be eliminated. And in order to defend herself—and him— against the possibility that she might attack him, she blanked him out of her consciousness. It seemed that Alex had re- sponded to his mother's pathology by being a "good baby" and being quiet and passive. And so it was a huge relief to me that as he took on a more positive role in his mother's mind, he also began to be livelier and more adventurous in the room. Alex became a regular part of our sessions because Jane could allow him to be with us. Regularly a period of "reverie" was initiated by Jane or Alex. We tried to imagine what Alex was communi- cating or feeling, and Alex rewarded his mother with more interaction. Gradually Jane's guilt diminished, enabling her to respond more positively. Mother and baby began to use toys together, and Jane bought Alex his first book. Proudly she dem- onstrated how he would sit on the floor next to her to look at it— they were moving towards each other. They began to have more eye contact, and Jane sometimes talked to Alex spontaneously, sometimes in a teasing way about me. Observing another person was becoming acceptable. Jane began to feel herself to be in a relationship with her baby. However, progress was fragile, and holiday breaks or other stressful events caused serious disrup- tion. Then we would go back to Alex sitting in the corner and Jane staring out of the window.

After a year's work with me Jane felt more confident and less anxious about being seen as a "bad" mother and began attend- ing a play-group with a close connection to the clinic. This time she was able to accept outside help with Alex. Because her inter- nal world was changing, she was able to empathize with her child. The other day she reported that in the play-group another child had been about to push Alex off the slide. She said, "I noticed this kid was a bit of a bully, and I heard your voice saying 'What's going on here?' and I said, 'Don't push my Alex, he's only little.' Before, I wouldn't have even noticed."

Theoretical considerations

The women I see are confused. They thought they wanted to have a baby, but this separate, demanding "other" with different needs from their own was neither what they wanted nor what they had imagined. Dinora Pines (1997) separates pregnancy, birth, and the postnatal relationship between mother and baby and sees "a marked distinction between the wish to become pregnant and the wish to bring a live baby into the world and become a mother" (p. 131). I too notice this distinction, which is expressed in the desire to be pregnant but which excludes the real baby. Instead, there are complex narcissistic phantasies that encapsulate the baby but do not undergo transformation as the reality of the pregnancy progresses.

Freud (1905d), a man of his time, declared that pregnancy and birth gratified every woman's basic desire. He thought that having a baby of her own would partially compensate for the unrealizable desire for a penis. Although in general I would not accept this, nonetheless there is something in what Freud said that strikes a chord. The women with whom I work seem to be acting out a retaliatory phantasy through the act of conception. In the normal process of a loving conception leading to a healthy pregnancy, there is the possibility of enrichment and development for the mother, the father, and the developing child. But for many women there is an impulse to solve a psychic problem magically, via a bodily event. This is not the fruitful meeting of sperm and ovum and the first step in the process of lovingly creating a child but, rather, a group of primitive phantasies attached to conception as a narcissistically gratifying event. There is triumph over the disappointing mother in favour of incorporating father's penis as a substitute breast that will be better and more satisfying than the breast that failed. These omnipotent phantasies obliterate the real experience of the pregnancy and the developing baby. This puts at risk the next stage of pregnancy, where a woman's process of identification with, and differentiation from, both the developing baby and her own mother enables "good-enough" maternal capacities and empathy to evolve. This process does not take place for this group of mothers.

So what happens in the experience of childbirth? For many of the women I see, the labour was a shocking event. The phantasy of the baby as an idealized reparative object is shattered by the onset of painful contractions that are felt to be initiated by an internal but alien presence. As a result the labour is problematic, and hi-tech medical intervention involving sado-masochistic encounters between patient and medical staff is common. This can be seen as another enactment of the woman's original trauma of "violent rupture" between mother and child. In the woman's mind the baby tears himself (or is torn by painful and frightening medical procedures) away from her, destroying her phantasy of omnipotent control. There is worse to follow. The baby's normal demands repeatedly trigger a debilitating cycle in the mother of loss of control followed by emotional with-drawal. Thus the baby relentlessly exposes the mother's original trauma and threatens to break down her defences.

Winnicott's famous phrase that "there is no such thing as a baby" advises us to consider the baby as part of "a nursing couple". He sees the good-enough mother creating a secure en-vironment—psychic and physical—from which the infant can emerge later as an individual into a world of object relations. For some of the mothers I am describing this is impossible. A traumatic childhood has left them psychically damaged and cut off from their objects. This disturbed pattern of object relating in the mother makes the trans-generational transmission of similar psychic damage inevitable. However, here I am describing two different kinds of trauma that perpetuate this failure between mother and baby.

First, there is the trauma of a "violent rupture" between mother and baby that is so evident in Jane's story. Here the baby feels torn away from the mother at a time when s/he is unable to survive the loss of mother's love. This loss can happen in many ways (and at different stages of development) but re-sults in the baby feeling ". . . in a state of acute confusion, or the agony of disintegration. They know what it is like to be dropped, to fall over, or to become split into psychosomatic disunion" (Winnicott, 1969, p. 260). This leaves the baby in an extremely vulnerable state from which it is hard to recover—particularly if, like Jane, there is the second kind of "cumulative trauma" (Khan, 1974) that is on-going. This manifests as a prolonged lack of sensitive emotional contact between mother and infant, which is just as traumatic as the "sudden rupture" for the child. Here the baby is repeatedly let down by a maternal object, with no reparative contact with a protecting paternal object. The lack of sustained secure maternal contact leaves the baby unable to regulate his affect or have a sense of himself in bodily terms. It also leads to difficulties in the infant's capacity to tolerate separateness or to have an awareness of what happens in another person's mind. Inevitably the baby learns to survive by creating a false-self personality that the mother can tolerate. It is noticeable that the babies I see, whose mothers are disturbed in this way, are often described as "good babies": they make very few demands, are quiet, and are often precociously self-reliant.

Conclusion

As children, women with disturbances in the postnatal period had suffered trauma that makes trans-generational transmission of the same kind of disturbances inevitable. Pregnancy is seen as a solution. The baby is phantasized as an idealized reparative object that in reality brings disaster to the mother. Having a baby reveals the mother's original trauma, making breakdown a possibility. To control destructive impulses, the mother banishes her baby from her mind, and the infant experiences an unavailable mother—a repetition of the mother's own trauma. Depression and a fear of damaging the baby irreparably brings the mother into treatment. Inevitably the psychotherapeutic relationship recreates the "ghosts" from the mother's past and enactments in the transference are inevitable.

However, I have found that working to establish a "normal projective identification" (Bion, 1962b) between the mother and myself enables the mother slowly to take back and manage her fears. When the mother feels contained by me, she is able to "give birth" to the baby in her mind, and then she and I and her baby work together to develop a motherliness of her own. Through this process feelings of hatred and destructiveness begin the long journey towards care and concern.

CHAPTER FIVE

The duty to care
and the need to split

Angela Foster

As a society we allocate the responsibility for caring for some of the most difficult and unlikeable people to specific groups of professionals. This responsibility gives rise to considerable anxiety, and some form of splitting may well be inevitable, even necessary, for self-preservation. The task of an organizational consultant is to challenge the splitting where it is deemed to be problematic for the protection of workers, clients, the agency, and the general public.

This chapter arises out of psychoanalytically oriented consultancy to teams of staff in the helping professions where there is a statutory "duty to care". It takes as its premise the seemingly paradoxical hypothesis that workers may need to split off part of their emotional experience in order to preserve their own mental health and provide reliable services to their clients. I use the word "paradoxical" because we are familiar with the therapeutic struggle to achieve depressive-position functioning that enables us to hold on to ambivalent feelings of love and hate and to sustain successful loving and caring relationships with others. In contrast, we think of paranoid–schizoid-position functioning as a state of mind in which we use the unconscious dynamics of splitting and projection to rid ourselves of conflict. These processes interfere with our ability to love and care for others and blind us to what is really going on in our relationships. It would therefore follow that in order to comply with a "duty to care", people in the helping professions should avoid splitting rather than view it as a professional necessity.

A case example

Imagine that you are the key worker for a young man of 26. He is strong and physically healthy although mentally disturbed. He can present as relaxed and easy-going, but you are aware that this masks extreme anxiety. He hears voices of a persecuting nature and often reacts in a paranoid manner. Sometimes you feel afraid of him, yet you also see in him a very needy and rather helpless little boy, and you want to mother him.

There are times when he—let's call him Mike—seems to think that you are simply "out to get him" and others when he seems to feel that he cannot live without you. He drifted into the city where you work some years ago, and you know little about his family. His present social relationships appear to be casual, stormy, and unreliable. His only stable relationships are with his professional workers. Mike is client of the local community mental health team, and you are his care manager (employed by the local social services department) or his community psychiatric nurse (employed by the local National Health Service Mental Health Trust). Mike meets the criteria to be taken on by your team because there are periods when he is clearly psychotic and requires hospital admission. He is seen by a psychiatrist every few months and receives medication from his G.P.

The most difficult aspects of Mike's behaviour are those connected with his personality disorder. He cannot be relied upon to take his prescribed medication responsibly, and he supplements this with illegal drugs. Mike is unpredictable and unreliable. Although a regular visitor to your agency, he rarely sticks to his appointment times, and sometimes you are relieved when he fails to keep an appointment. No one in your team is very hopeful that he will "get better". If he manages to stay alive into middle age, then he might quieten down, but you doubt that he will ever find much satisfaction in life.

You are stuck with him and if, while in a rage, he attacks and kills another person, the subsequent inquiry may find you guilty of "failing in your duty to care", placing your career at risk.

This frightening scenario is one that haunts professionals working in community care of the mentally ill and others working in child protection or with clients who, while not deemed to be mentally ill, present a risk to themselves or others.
   We need to ask ourselves:

• What would constitute good-enough care for someone like Mike?
• What are the pitfalls for professional staff?

What would constitute good-enough care?

Clients like Mike want to be helped in that they want to be relieved of their pain. However, they appear to have little desire to take part in a relationship in which their pain would be addressed with a view to thinking about it and understanding it. Rather, Mike is the kind of patient of whom Steiner (1993) wrote:

> The priority for the patient is to get rid of unwanted mental contents, which he projects into the analyst, and in these states he is able to take very little back into his mind. He does not have the time or the space to think, and he is afraid to examine his own mental processes. Words are used, not primarily to convey information, but as actions having an

effect on the analyst, and the analyst's words are likewise felt as actions indicating something about the analyst's state of mind rather than offering insight to the patient.

This form of psychic equilibrium is maintained by warding off any communication, which might, if taken in and considered, disrupt the status quo by providing food for thought. Clients like Mike often say things like, "You're only saying that because . . .", "You just want me to . . .", or "Why are you doing this to me?" They tend (and one might even say unconsciously choose) to view every communication as a manipulation. Their internal worlds are filled with part-object relationships in which people use each other.

Steiner (1993) used the term "psychic retreat" to describe the unconscious processes whereby people with borderline personality disorders avoid both the pain of persecutory anxiety felt in the paranoid–schizoid position and the pain of depressive anxiety felt in the depressive position. A mental life in a psychic retreat—though static—is experienced as preferable to a life of overwhelming anxieties with feared catastrophic consequences. Some clients may appear to exist in a stuck and unchanging state, while others, like Mike, are more volatile.

> In less stuck situations, which of course occur in patients who may nevertheless be quite ill, and even psychotic, more movement is discernible and shifts occur in which anxieties are at least transiently faced (Steiner, 1993, p. 88).

There were clearly times when Mike was filled with persecutory anxiety. He behaved as if everyone was out to get him, he complained bitterly about the inadequacy or the inappropriateness of the treatment he received, and he could be very threatening to those around him. You were afraid of him and you worried that he might attack someone.

Occasionally he was remorseful. His life experience is one of being left, and he was touched by your commitment to him, becoming aware of how much you meant to him. At these times perhaps he could imagine how difficult and unpleasant he was to be with and unconsciously feared that he may have damaged you and that he would lose you. This filled him with self-loathing and depressive anxiety, which felt too much for him to bear, and you became afraid that he would kill himself. This feeling persisted until he flipped back into his retreat of moaning about his predicament while doing nothing to change it. After all—as Mike saw it—it was your responsibility, not his, and if you were any good at your job, he would not have been feeling like this.

Both Mike and you had to steer a careful path between these two extremes of anxiety. When you felt too distant or were unavailable to him, he felt abandoned, left alone to manage or not manage his persecutory feelings. In contrast, times of true emotional closeness between you and him gave rise to claustrophobic anxieties because through your ability to be in touch with his experience he was put in touch with the pain of his life. When this felt unbearable, the "in-touchness" was experienced as persecuting, and consequently Mike rebuffed, rejected, or attacked you, his sensitive worker. In this manner he hurt you, engendering feelings of hate. Britton writes:

> the claustrophobic–agoraphobic dilemma, which Henri Rey (1979) pointed out is characteristic of the borderline phenomenon, a deathly container, or exposure in a shattered world. . . . Faced with these two catastrophic alternatives, incarceration or fragmentation, some people . . . remain paralysed at the frontier, on the threshold. [Britton, 1992, p. 89]

Caring for someone involves activities such as the ability to be emotionally in touch with the other person as a whole person, a readiness to consider their pain and their needs and act accordingly, and a desire to make up for any pain we may have caused them. We do not usually equate this with duty. However, in the professional context a "duty to care" reminds us that we owe this to all our clients—even those who are not the sort of people towards whom we naturally feel any warmth.

In the case of clients like Mike, we are required to form caring relationships with people who are rarely able to reciprocate. We have to manage ourselves and our ambivalent feelings without resorting to projection or retaliation, at the same time managing that which is projected into us by our clients. Our job is to give back a sense of reality and substance to people who, through continuous processes of projection, feel unreal and empty. This has to be done in a manner that the client can tolerate—we have to be able to judge what the client is able to tolerate and contain at any given time and formulate our interventions accordingly. The "duty to care" also implies a degree of risk management to ensure that both the clients and those around them are safe, and a degree of risk-taking if the client is to live independently in the community. It requires the worker to be in touch with the client's level of disturbance, including their pain, despair, and destructiveness, while at the same time being sufficiently detached from the client to assess the situation on a regular basis. In addition, we need to be capable of recognizing those times when physical containment—hospital admission, either voluntary or compulsory—is necessary. Often we have to find ways of being alive to and emotionally in touch with what the client wishes to remain ignorant of.

What are the pitfalls for professional staff?

Essentially, the pitfalls for staff are found in the ways *we* have of remaining ignorant of what we could know but would prefer not to know. Bion (1967) stated that "For a proper understanding of the situation when attacks on linking are being delivered it is useful to postulate thoughts that have no thinker." Bollas (1987) referred to things that remain locked away in seemingly inaccessible places in our minds as "unthought knowns", and Steiner (1993) described the psychic process of "turning a blind eye" as a way of not seeing those things that we fear are too uncomfortable to face.

We all know what it is like to want to be with our clients and to want to avoid them: to love them and to hate them. This experience presents us with emotional conflict and therefore emotional pain of our own and puts us in danger of swinging between persecutory anxiety, with its accompanying paranoia and deadening despair, and depressive anxiety, with its guilt and accompanying dangers of manic over-involvement and omnipotence. When we find ourselves on this sort of emotional roller-coaster, we lose confidence in our professional skills and thereby experience even more persecutory or depressive anxiety, as we fear that we are not functioning well.

Persecutory anxiety

Persecutory anxiety may cause us to overlook our clients' good points while projecting all the bad things into them. When we do this, we are more likely to busily manage our clients in order to keep the destructiveness in check at the same time as minimizing our personal involvement. This approach may achieve some success in risk-avoidance when clients are "managed" in the sense of being monitored, but as workers lose their humanity, so clients lose the opportunity of meaningful relationships. Britton (1992) described the client's experience of workers employing these defences thus:

> The belief that they are dealing with an impermeable object coated with an impregnable sense of superiority drives some personalities to violence. It underlies a good many of the situations of spiralling violence which occur in professional situations, whether in psychiatry, or social work or teaching, or in psychoanalysis.... In other people or at other times, the sense of being faced with an impervious object induces an acquiescent despair. [Britton, 1992, p. 91]

To retreat from emotional involvement with difficult clients is both a form of self-protection and a danger. In retreating we cease to hold the client in mind as a whole person, and we become deadened to the unconscious communication, running the risk of not seeing what we need to see and consequently of not doing what we should be doing. *Individuals* who tend to work in this way are a problem to a well-functioning team, and effective managers will address this with the individual concerned. While I have no first-hand experience of *teams* working like this, it is not uncommon to hear one team describe another in these terms. For example, a community team might describe the team on the in-patient ward as spending all day in the office filling in forms instead of talking to their patients. While this sort of communication may have elements of reality, it also contains elements of projection, as usually workers wish to disown their desire to avoid their clients. The understandable relief that is expressed by members of a community team when one of their most difficult clients is held either in hospital or in prison is also an indication of their—possibly long felt but unacknowledged— desire to be rid of, distant from, and protected from that person.

Depressive anxiety

Depressive anxiety leads us to find different ways of splitting off part of our experience, often colluding with our clients by focusing on the good aspects of the relationship while overlooking their destructiveness. This leads to sentimentalized client relationships.

Workers who choose to work in teams with the specific task of caring for some of the most damaged and damaging people in our society do so because they want to see the good in these people. They want to provide their clients with choices and opportunities that have been denied to them elsewhere, believing that they will benefit from such care and attention. They are rightly concerned about the stigmatization that comes from labelling others, yet unless they can bear to see the destructiveness in these clients, they are putting themselves, their clients, and others at risk. In a paper entitled "Thinking about Risk" (Foster, 1998b) I describe events that culminated in a fire in a residential unit and in repeated break-ins in a day centre. These events might not have reached such terrible crisis-points if the staff groups had allowed themselves to be in touch with the hatred—which both they and their clients were feeling—at an earlier stage.

Tom Main (1968) described how some senior staff failed to acknowledge the destructive aspects of their rather "special" patients. These dedicated nurses took their patients' lack of improvement as evidence that they had not done enough for them. While resenting colleagues for being harsh and withholding, these nurses omnipotently believed that their ever-increasing personal involvement was what would succeed. They continued in this way until their own serious ill health prevented them from continuing.

Particularly perverse clients will abuse their workers with their relentless demands and seductiveness and with their refusal to benefit from all the attention devoted to them. It is important that we see this, because if we get caught up in the process, it is to the detriment of all concerned.

In these examples the persecutory or depressive anxieties that workers find unbearable cause them to resort to forms of splitting that then affect their relationships with their clients. Cardona (1999) commented on a "flatness", a rude or polite passivity she experiences in staff teams, which changes only when team members are willing to express their hatred and feel they have permission to do so. When they describe how angry they feel about the way certain clients treat them, team members come to life and are once again able to think about their clients.

The culture of blame

A further source of anxiety for workers is the manner in which their professional duty to care is addressed by their organizations and by society at large. Clients are provided with networks of care and receive input from multi-disciplinary groups of professionals. In the context of effective client management and therapeutic understanding, workers meet and work together in groups (sometimes with the client present), making decisions on care plans and treatment. Yet the focus of complaints procedures, investigations, and inquiries is on individual workers, and this sets up a culture that runs counter to teamwork and cuts across it. Individuals are called to make confidential statements about their work and that of their colleagues, and the emphasis is on the individual as personally accountable rather than on the individual as a team player.

Gwen Wright, in an unpublished essay entitled "To what extent is the law of tort an appropriate mechanism for deterring blameworthy conduct?", argues that "Whatever its efficacy in other fields, tort may be unhelpful *psychologically* in deterring poor practice in healthcare." She adds that investigating the actions of individuals is inappropriate when a client has been cared for by a clinical team that has made decisions based on a number of complex variables over a period of time. In these circumstances "tort liability may miss careless behaviour and direct attention to the avoidance of liability rather than the promotion of good practice". There is no shortage of evidence to support this view. At a personal level, workers are distressed to report that when they hear of a client's death, their first thought is whether their notes are up to date. At an organizational level, bureaucratic monitoring invades supervision time, destroying the possibilities for more reflective case discussion, and while we can all agree that inquiries provide opportunities to learn from mistakes, it is almost impossible to have such a discussion in a team. In these instances the persecutory anxiety (the contained) may shatter the meeting (the container). Our experience or our fear of a shattered container puts us in paranoid–schizoid mode, and further splitting becomes inevitable. Fear of persecution forces us to turn away from multi-disciplinary discussions towards more private and closed two-person relationships in which both clients and workers are at times the "doers" and at times the "done to".

The need to split

To summarize: anxiety arising from direct work with clients fuels a desire to split—that is, a desire to turn away from awareness of aspects of the work that increase our levels of discomfort. An external culture of blame, which seeks to apportion blame and individualize failure, produces even greater levels of anxiety, with the result that individuals are even more likely to resort to splitting as a defence against the pain of this experience. When the anxiety level in teams is such that the contained (the anxiety) shatters the container (whatever form of meeting is intended to help workers process their anxiety and think about their work), this gives rise to social, organizational defences that shore up the fragile social care system, acting as pseudo-containers for the work. While policies and procedures form a necessary part of the structure in which the client work takes place, they are not containers of anxiety. Containment is an emotional process, which is disrupted by these mechanical procedures rather than supported by them. Yet from central government downwards a whole series of bureaucratic policies and procedures have been put into place as a way of trying to address public anxiety, and the demand is to eliminate rather than think about the unavoidable and inevitable element of risk in work of this kind.

So far as the workers are concerned, we can see how an external bureaucratic social defence system may appear to be both necessary and effective as it suits workers to split off aspects of their awareness in order to establish an emotional distance that will support a workable routine. Thus the prospect of a social defence system that numbs the feelings and allows the possibility of "going through the motions" more mechanically brings relief.

Lest we assume that such modes of functioning are limited to disturbed individuals and social care organizations, Hoggett (1992) draws our attention to a societal tendency to turn a blind eye to hatred and mass destructiveness through a process of a "routinization of everyday life". He reminds us that "No one is free from the solace that bad sense and nonsense bring; these little lies we tell ourselves seem so preferable to the pain of thought." He also quotes Bion (1962b) who observed: "the way in which we take for granted the routines of everyday life" which preserve "an attitude of mindlessness" in the service of providing "a stable form of containment for going on being".

Social defence systems are a way of maintaining a status quo. However, while providing us with relief from the roller-coaster of emotion arising from alternating persecutory and depressive anxieties, they keep us static, hindering us from moving on. In addition, the effort involved in the struggle to stay in one spot wears us out. If we need these defences, we also need some sort of antidote to their side effects. In short, social defence systems are pathological, but they may also be necessary. However, if we can achieve a fluidity of movement between operating within the defensive system and in the depressive position, the defences—or one might say organizational retreats—may be more like benign ponds than like stagnant or malignant backwaters.

The struggle for integration

The usual way of facilitating depressive-position functioning, which involves a reintegration of what has been split off, is to provide a variety of "reflective spaces"—quiet, uninterrupted spaces within the working week that are capable of containing and modifying the personal and collective anxieties. By reflecting on the emotional factors, including transference and countertransference, in our work, we hope to reach a greater understanding of the issues affecting our clients, and this then informs our subsequent interventions. Opportunities for this may be available on training courses, but more usually people find them in individual and group supervision, in case discussions, and in staff support groups.

However, when the level of persecutory anxiety increases in an agency, the chances of the contained (the anxiety) shattering the container (the meeting) increases. One consequence of this might be that the "in-house" reflective spaces become invaded and contaminated by the organizational socially defensive routines of checking up on things as a way of "covering the organizational back". In more extreme situations, these spaces are destroyed completely, often without any noticeable protest, because when we feel overwhelmed by persecutory anxiety, our ability to share openly with our colleagues suffers, and our desire for discussion diminishes. Supervision sessions may be cancelled altogether, and groups are badly attended, leaving those who do attend struggling with the task of thinking about what is happening to the team as a whole.

In such circumstances it helps if there is an external consult-ant—someone who is not caught up in the day-to-day dynamics of the workplace and who, in Hoggett's (1992) words, can act as "the apparatus for thinking that which otherwise cannot be thought". The first bit of apparatus that is needed in these circumstances is an intact physical container, and it is the con-sultant's job to re-establish the boundaries and the task of the meeting, thus recreating and protecting the setting for the work. The consultant can then take up the third position in relation to the agency and its clients, with the aim of enabling the group to struggle with the reflective task of standing back and looking at what is happening in the team and with their clients. When this struggle—the process of containing the anxieties—is successful, people regain their ability to hold onto painful, ambivalent feel-ings and are able to feel in touch with themselves and with their work.

However, as the following case examples demonstrate, in extreme circumstances reintegration may lead to acute emo-tional pain, giving rise to further splitting or shattering of the container.

Example one

A consultant was contracted to work with a team of child-care workers that had been subject to an inquiry following the death of a young child through parental neglect. The death of a child is always particularly painful, and there is a natural tendency to look for someone to blame. In this case, the workers who had a statutory "duty to care" certainly felt blamed and in some ways also felt blameworthy. Through providing consultation, the agency was offering this team some help with managing their feelings. Initially the consultant was asked to make times available at her place of work—not theirs—for anyone who wished to take up the offer of individual sessions, and she proposed that in due course she would offer times when the team could meet as a group.

Sessions away from the workplace meant that confidentiality was guaranteed, and this appeared to provide a strong enough container for individual workers to work on personal issues in relation to the events that had led to this child's death. However, as the work progressed, the consultant began to feel increasingly overlooked and neglected: her invoices were not paid, and she was unsuccessful in her efforts to contact the manager. One way of thinking about this is to hypothesize that what could be contained and addressed individually, in private, and away from the workplace could not be owned or acknowledged collectively by management within the organization. In a misguided attempt to protect the organizational container, the link between it and the work—taking place elsewhere—was attacked. This could also be viewed as a desire to locate the pain of being in touch personally in the individual workers while protecting the organization from a more appropriate but feared collective "intouchness". The consultant felt that having become a repository for the awful, personal, and often sordid details of the case, she was being cut adrift from the organizational lifeline for fear of contamination. Possibly these dynamics mirrored some of the dynamics between the baby and its parents as well as between the family and the agency.

It seemed to the consultant that her task was twofold. She had to demonstrate that the consultancy could survive these unconscious attacks, and she had to have the group meetings she had proposed as a way of indicating that it was possible to integrate this work back into the team and into the organization. In other words, her unstated but clearly assigned task was to reassure those involved that there was a way of *collectively* examining the details of the case, learning from the process and surviving the experience. This process was extremely painful, yet it succeeded in fostering a greater awareness and understanding between team members, and the consultant was eventually paid for her work.

However, shortly afterwards the department was reorganized and the team dispersed. I would also suggest that this —like many other reorganizations—was an organizational defence against living with the pain of the experience and with the knowledge of what had gone wrong. Instead of being clearly cited and sighted within the midst of the organization, this awareness was pushed to the back of people's minds as they began to adjust and adapt to their new circumstances.

Example two

What workers prefer not to think about may be experienced as a sort of toxic waste that is then projected into the consultant. In these circumstances a desire to sack the consultant might be thought of as a desire to expel the danger.

- One team whose members were very committed to adapting to their clients needs said they wanted the consultant to adapt her methods to suit them. Her response was to acknowledge that while they might wish to find someone else for the work, she was committed to her method of working. This was a thoughtful and genuine response, but it felt risky to say it, and in doing so she outraged some team members. However, this led to a useful discussion about how difficult it was for this team to acknowledge and value differences between themselves and to wonder about whether they might undervalue themselves and their clients by attempting to "be all things to all people".

- A consultant's unavoidable lateness for a meeting with one staff group prompted a vicious attack on her lack of boundaries, her lack of professionalism, and her unsuitability for the job. In the event all she could do was to question why they were being so unforgiving. The mood of the group then changed, as team members felt remorseful and shocked by the level of their hatred towards her. Subsequently they were able to consider this in the light of their anxieties about failing in their struggle to provide a reliable and professional service to their suffering yet destructive and, at times, hated clients.

The task of the staff support group in these two agencies was to think about the issues the confrontation raised, reintegrating the splits and bearing the depressive anxiety in the service of developing more effective and realistic responses to their clients.

Containment in working groups

If we take the view that people and organizations need their defences and that consultants have a responsibility to support people in their work, then we have to act sensitively so as not to upset the defensive status quo too much, at the same time as trying to ensure that there is a fluidity of movement between paranoid–schizoid- and depressive-position functioning. In this conceptual system the staff support group represents one place (though not the only one) where people can touch a depressive position base.

It would be nice to think that the whole team got together for what was collectively felt to be an important part of the team's task, but this is rarely the case. Staff are absent through leave, sickness, and crises. In some teams some members regularly attend the staff support group while others choose not to. I have come to think that in these cases those who value this sort of work and feel able to do it are working on issues on behalf of the team as a whole. It does not mean that those who attend are the best workers or that those who don't are the worst. They are merely different, and there are people in both groups who are better at the work than others.

So, how does this work? An effective staff support group will have a clear boundary, which aims to keep the details of who said what about whom confidential to the group. In this way a split is managed. However, in order to bring about some form of reintegration within the team as a whole, support group members must also take responsibility for thoughtful reporting to staff meetings on those issues that the support group deems need further consideration.

There will also be times within the life of a team when the sickness level in the team or avoidance of the staff support group needs consideration in the group. For example, when the work of a team, and in particular the work of specific team members, is being investigated, individuals who are singled out feel very exposed. They may decide to let the support group know that they feel too vulnerable to attend. Group members then have to struggle with this information, together with their own anxiety about the nature of the investigation and their fears about its conclusions.

We all have views about what constitutes a failure in the "duty to care" and may be critical of the practice of our colleagues, yet we can also empathize with someone who is under investigation. In these circumstances the task of the group is to think about the effect of the investigation on particular colleagues and on the team as a whole. Only when this is done can the group attend to its primary task—that of addressing those detailed aspects of the team's work *which team members know need investigating but tend not to think about.*

REFERENCES

Baranger, M. (1993). The mind of the analyst: from listening to interpretation. *International Journal of Psycho-Analysis, 74*: 15–24.

Barrows, P. (2000). Making the case for dedicated infant mental health services. *Psychoanalytic Psychotherapy, 14* (2): 111–128.

Bion, W. R. (1962a). *Learning from Experience*. Reprinted London: Karnac Books, 1991.

Bion, W. R. (1962b). A theory of thinking. *International Journal of Psycho-Analysis, 43*: 306–310.

Bion, W. R. (1967). *Second Thoughts. Selected Papers on Psychoanalysis*. Reprinted London: Karnac Books, 1987.

Bollas, C. (1987). *The Shadow of the Object: Psychoanalysis of the Unthought Known*. London: Free Association Books.

Brenneis, C. (1994). Observations on psychoanalytic listening. *Psychoanalytic Quarterly, 63*: 29.

Britton, R. (1992). Keeping things in mind. In: R. Anderson (Ed.), *Clinical Lectures on Klein and Bion* (pp. 102–113). London and New York: Tavistock/Routledge.

Brown, G., & Harris, T. (1978). *Social Origins of Depression*. London: Tavistock.

Cardona, F. (1999). The team as a sponge: how the nature of the task affects the behaviour and mental life of a team. In: R. French & R. Vince (Ed.), *Group Relations, Management and Organisation* (pp. 239–250). Oxford: Oxford University Press.

Coulter, H., & Loughlin, E. (1999). Synergy of verbal and non verbal therapies in the treatment of the mother–infant relationship. *British Journal of Psychotherapy, 16* (1): 58–73.

Cramer, B. (1993). Are postpartum depressions a mother–infant relationship disorder? *Infant Mental Health Journal, 14* (4), 283–297.

Cramer, B. (1997). Psychodynamic perspectives on the treatment of postpartum depression. In: L. Murray & P. Cooper (Eds.), *Postpartum Depression and Child Development*. New York/London: The Guildford Press.

Davenloo, H. (1995). *Unlocking the Unconscious*. Chichester/New York: Wiley.

Daws, D. (1989). *Through the Night. Helping Parents and Sleepless Infants*. London: Free Association Books.

Daws, D. (1993). Feeding problems and relationship difficulties: therapeutic work with parents and infants. *Journal of Child Psychotherapy, 19* (2): 5–17.

Etchegoyen, H. (1991). *The Fundamentals of Psychoanalytic Technique* (pp. 512–514). London: Karnac Books.

Faimberg, H. (1992). The countertransference position and the countertransference. *International Journal of Psycho-Analysis, 73*: 541–546.

Ferenczi, S. (1919). On the technique of psychoanalysis. *Further Contributions to the Theory and Technique of Psycho-Analysis*. New York: Basic Books.

Foster, A. (1989a). Psychotic processes and community care: the difficulty in finding the third position. In: A. Foster & V. Z. Roberts (Eds.), *Managing Mental Health in the Community: Chaos and Containment* (pp. 61–70). London/New York: Routledge.

Foster, A. (1989b). Thinking about risk. In: A. Foster & V. Z. Roberts (Ed.), *Managing Mental Health in the Community: Chaos and Containment* (pp. 84–94). London/New York: Routledge.

Fraiberg, S. H., Adelson, E., & Shapiro, U. (1975). Ghosts in the nursery: a psychoanalytical approach to the problem of impaired infant–mother relationship. *Journal of the American Academy of Child Psychiatry, 14*: 387–422.

Freedman, N. (1983). On psychoanalytic listening. *Psychoanalytic Contemporary Thought, 6*: 405–434.

Freud, S. (1905d). *Three Essays on the Theory of Sexuality and Other Works. Standard Edition, 7.*

Freud, S. (1905e [1901]). Fragment of an analysis of a case of hysteria. (1905). *Standard Edition, 7:* 1–122.

Freud, S. (1912e). Recommendations to physicians practising psychoanalysis. *Standard Edition, 12:* 102–120.

Freud, S. (1913c). On beginning the treatment: further recommendations on the technique of psycho-analysis. *Standard Edition, 12.*

Freud, S. (1926d [1925]). *Inhibitions, Symptoms and Anxiety. Standard Edition, 20.*

Gill, M. (1988). Converting psychotherapy into psychoanalysis. *Contemporary Psychoanalysis, 24:* 262–274.

Harvie-Clark, J. (1991). Counselling, psychotherapy, psychoanalysis: a personal perspective. *Bulletin of the British Association of Psychotherapists, 22:* 84–95.

Hoggett, P. (1992). *Partisans in an Uncertain World: The Psychoanalysis of Engagement.* London: Free Association Books.

Holmes, J. (1998). The changing aims of psychoanalytical psychotherapy—an integrative perspective. *International Journal of Psycho-Analysis, 79:* 227–240.

Hopkins, J. (1992). Infant–parent psychotherapy. *Journal of Child Psychotherapy, 18:* 5–17.

Keller, A. (1984). Planned brief psychotherapy in clinical practice. *British Journal of Medical Psychology, 57:* 347–361.

Khan, M. R. (1974). Dread of surrender to resourceless dependence in the analytic situation. In: *The Privacy of the Self.* London: Hogarth Press.

Klein, J. (1995). *Doubts and Certainties in the Practice of Psychotherapy.* London: Karnac Books.

Klein, J. (1998). Assessment: Who for? What for? *British Journal of Psychotherapy, 15:* 333–345.

Laplanche, J., & Pontalis, J.-B. (1973). *Language of Psychoanalysis.* London: Hogarth. Reprinted London: Karnac Books, 1988.

Main, T. (1968). The ailment. In: *The Ailment and Other Psychoanalytic Essays,* ed. J. Johns (pp. 12–35). London: Free Association Books.

Makari, G., & Shapiro, T. (1993). On psychoanalytic listening: language and unconscious communication. *Journal of the American Psychoanalytic Association, 41:* 991–1020.

Mander, G. (1995). In praise of once-a-week work. *British Journal of Psychotherapy, 12:* 3–14.

Mitchell, J. (2000). *Mad Men and Medusas Reclaiming Hysteria and the Effects of Sibling Relations on the Human Condition.* London: Allen Lane/The Penguin Press.

Naylor-Smith, A. (1994). Counselling and psychotherapy, is there a difference? *Counselling (BAC Journal), 8:* 284–286.

Ogden, T. H. (1996). Reconsidering three aspects of psychoanalytic technique. *International Journal of Psycho-Analysis, 77:* 883–900.

Perelberg, R. Jozef (Ed.) (1999). *Psychoanalytic Understanding of Violence and Suicide.* Routledge: London.

Pines, D. (1997). The relevance of early psychic development to pregnancy and abortion. In: J. Raphael-Leff & R. Jozef Perelberg (Eds.), *Female Experience.* London: Routledge.

Raphael-Leff, J. (1991). *Psychological Processes of Childbearing.* London: Chapman & Hall.

Rey, H. (1979). Schizoid phenomena in the borderline. In: J. Le Boit & A. Capponi (Eds.), *Advances in the Psychotherapy of the Borderline Patient* (pp. 449–484). New York: Jason Aronson. Also in E. Bott Spillius (Ed.), *Melanie Klein Today, Vol. 1: Mainly Theory* (pp. 203–229). London: Routledge, 1988.

Rogers, C. (1951). *Client-Centred Therapy.* London: Constable.

Rosenfeld, H. (1971). A clinical approach to the psycho-analytical theory of the life and death instincts: an investigation into the aggressive aspects of narcissism. *International Journal of Psycho-Analysis, 52:* 169–178.

Rycroft, C. (1968). *Critical Dictionary of Psychoanalysis.* London: Nelson. Reprinted London: Penguin, 1972.

Rycroft, C. (1995). On beginning treatment. *British Journal of Psychotherapy, 11:* 541–521.

Searles, H. F. (1979). *Countertransference and Related Subjects.* New York: International Universities Press.

Segal, H. (1981). Countertransference. In: *Delusion and Artistic Creativity & Other Psychoanalytic Essays.* New York/London: Jason Aronson.

Sifneos, P. E. (1972). *Short-term Psychotherapy and Emotional Crisis.* Cambridge, MA: Harvard University Press.

Steiner, J. (1993). *Psychic Retreats: Pathological Organisations in Psychotic, Neurotic and Borderline Patients.* London/New York: Routledge.

Stern, D. (1985). *The Interpersonal World of the Infant.* New York: Basic Books.

Welldon, E. V. (1988). *Mother, Madonna, Whore—The Idealisation and Denigration of Motherhood.* London: Guildford Press.

Winnicott, D. W. (1960). The theory of the parent–child relationship. In: *The Maturational Processes in the Facilitating Environment.* London: Hogarth, 1965.

Winnicott, D. W. (1964). *The Child the Family and the Outside World.* London: Penguin.

Winnicott, D.W. (1969). The mutuality of mother–infant experience. In C. Winnicott, R. Shepherd, & M. Davis (Eds.), *Psycho-Analytic Explorations.* London: Karnac Books, 1989.

Wright, K. (1991). *Vision and Separation Between Mother and Baby.* London: Free Association Books.

INDEX

fear, 11, 16, 65
Ferenczi, S., 49
Foster, A., vii, xi, 85–101
Fraiberg, S. H., 62
Fraser, L., viii, x, 23
free association, defining concept
    of psychoanalysis, 48
Freedman, N., 50
free-floating attention, 49–50
frequency of sessions (*passim*):
    Etchegoyen on, 47
    Freud on, 24, 27, 46
Freud, S., 11, 17, 68
    on dreams, 48, 59
    on free-floating (evenly
        suspended) attention, 49–
        50
    on frequency of sessions, 24, 27,
        46–48
    on pregnancy and birth, 81
    on repetition, 13
    on psychoanalysis:
        key concepts of, 48
        sound practice in, 47
        successful treatment in, 47
    use of couch by, 37

Gill, M., 47, 48, 54
Goldwyn, M., viii, x, 23
greed, 20, 65
    and psychoanalysis, 11
guilt, 13, 64, 68, 72, 80, 90
    acknowledgement of, in
        therapy, 12, 20
    mother's, 77
    repetition of in therapy, 13

Haque, S., viii, x, 23
Harris, T., 63
Harvie-Clark, J., 27, 28
hate, 11, 85, 89
history, patient's, 26
Hoggett, P., 95, 97

holding, 14, 51–55
    as containing, 15
Holmes, J., 28
Hopkins, J., 72
hunger, 11

"ideas of reference", 21
identification(s):
    of mother:
        with baby, 81
        projective, with analyst, 83
    unconscious, 55
interpretation, 8, 55, 58, 70
    dangers in, 20
    defining concept of
        psychoanalysis, 48
    and healing, 15
    reassurance formulated as, 47
    of separation between sessions,
        51
    and suggestion, 17
    techniques of, confronting,
        anxiety-provoking
        [Davenloo], 26
    transference, 73
    of unconscious contents, 51
inter-subjective third [Ogden], 29

Jung, C. G., 11

Keller, A., 28
Khan, M. R., 79, 83
Klein, J., vii, viii, x, 1–22, 23
Klein, M., 11

Laplanche, J., 48
libidinal wish, 48
listening:
    analytic, 50, 54–58
    "listening to listening"
        [Faimberg], 54–55
London Centre for Psychotherapy,
    ix